Never Give Up!

THE FRUIT OF LONGSUFFERING

NANCY MISSLER

KHW

Never Give Up!

Copyright 2005 by Nancy Missler

Published by The King's High Way Ministries, Inc.
P.O. Box 3111
Coeur d'Alene ID 83816
(866) 775-5464
www.kingshighway.org

Second printing, November, 2009

ISBN: 978-0-9760994-1-3

Scripture quotations are from the King James Version
of the Holy Bible.

PRINTED IN THE UNITED STATES OF AMERICA

Never Give Up!
Table of Contents

*He <u>never</u> let go, He <u>never</u> gave in, and
He <u>never</u> gave up!*

The Empty Tomb

2005 Israel Tour

"We are troubled on every side, *yet not distressed*; we are perplexed, *but not in despair*; persecuted, *but not forsaken*; cast down, *but not destroyed...*"
(2 Corinthians 4:8-9)

**"He who hath begun a good work in you will perform it until the day of Jesus Christ."
(Philippians 1:6)**

Introduction

What do you *do* when your dreams, your plans and your hopes blow up in your face? Who do you blame when everything in the Bible gave you hope but, then, out of the blue, all was destroyed? How do you react when difficult and trying circumstances seem to go on and on and on?

Have you ever experienced such a time as this? A time where you became so confused, so discouraged and so disheartened in your Christian walk that you wanted to let go, give in and give up?

The dictionary describes this feeling of utter disillusionment as *dismay*. It means we have become so perplexed, bewildered and confused at the total devastation we see in our lives that we are completely undone. The dictionary describes it this way: *Dismay occurs when courage and resolution are taken away from us by the alarm and fear we find at every turn.*

Synonyms of the word *dismay* are: appalled, horrified, disheartened, disabled, unnerved or cracked. It's the feeling of just *wanting to give up and die.* How aptly these words express Job's state of mind when, after all the devastation in his life, he cries out "now, I am nothing!" (Job 6:21)

If we are honest with ourselves, all of us at one time or another have felt dismay. However in many Christian lives, this state of mind seems to be the "norm." Many have experienced some sort of vision, dream or hope smashed in front of their eyes and have been left in an impossible situation. (Proverbs 29:18; 13:12) They not only feel deceived by God, but abandoned by Him in their greatest need. The desperation that results is beyond any sensory pain that one could ever bear. Psychiatrists tell us that grief of mind *is* often harder to bear than physical pain. Paul expresses it perfectly in 2 Corinthians 1:8 when he says that he "despaired of life itself."

As Christians, *hope* in God and the promises of His Word are the anchors of our soul. (Hebrews 6: 19) It's imperative that we have complete confidence that the Lord *will do* all that He promises in His Word. That's the basis of our faith. Our spiritual existence is determined by our expectation of the Lord's provision for our future. Consequently, if our trust and expectations are shattered by some inexplicable experience, then overwhelming fear and confusion and the feeling of wanting to give up result.

Take, for example, the young Christian woman who has undergone three open heart surgeries in the last three years. Cindy not only was assured by her doctor each time that she was healed and could go home, but she also has had many personal promises from the Lord about her healing. How does Cindy now deal with the fact that, as of today, her heart is once again 98% blocked and, she now faces her 29th angioplasty in 36 months?

Then, there's the Christian wife, married for over 30 years, who not only has had hundreds of personal Scriptures promising the restoration of her marriage, but also the word of her wayward husband that "this time" he would remain faithful. How does she now deal with the fact that once again her husband has been caught cheating?

And, again, how does the Christian husband apply God's promise of Psalm 91 *to give His angels charge over him and to keep him in all his ways*, when one year ago he lost his only daughter in a tragic car accident, his only son, soon after, was committed to a long-term care unit because of drug use and today his wife lies in a hospital because of an attempted suicide.

In light of these trials, tribulations and tragedies, how does one keep from becoming dismayed, discouraged and depressed? How do we avoid the feeling of wanting to let go, give in and give up?

This is the kind of scenario that seems to be happening in so many Christian homes at the present time. As one believer put it to me recently: "It's like being on a bungee cord, bounced back and forth, never able to stop." Another expressed it this way: "It's like bringing a baby to birth [meaning God's own personal promises], but not being able to deliver it (promises unfulfilled)." And yet another: "I don't know how much more I can take. I'm just about ready to give up!"

The question becomes: How do we refrain from being angry, bitter and blaming God in situations like these? How do we get to the point where we *never let go, never give in and never give up?*

Isaiah 41:10 tells us, "Fear thou not; for I am with thee. *Be not dismayed* [**never give up**]; for I am thy God. I will strengthen thee; yea, I will help thee; yea, I will uphold thee with the right hand of my righteousness." (See also Deuteronomy 31:8)

There's our promise. There's our hope. And there's our part. God is telling us that if we choose *not* to be dismayed, then He will be with us, He will strengthen us, help us and uphold us!

The question is: How do we do this? How do *we* never give up, so that *He* will be with us, help us and uphold us?

Longsuffering

The Biblical answer is by learning *longsuffering*. And, believe it or not, longsuffering is a fruit of the Spirit. Galatians 5:22 lists it as number 4 on a list of 10!! Now, all of us yearn for the fruit of Love, joy, peace, gentleness, goodness, faith, meekness and temperance, but who on earth wants to learn "longsuffering" or patient enduring? No, thank you! And, yet, God says longsuffering *is* a part of His character, a part of His image and a part of His nature. Therefore it's something He wants us all to learn.

Paul tells us in 1 Timothy 1:16 that he, himself, is a perfect pattern or model of Christ's longsuffering. He says that since Christ patiently endured his (Paul's), sinful ways, we must remember this example and patiently endure others' sinful ways.

Longsuffering simply means "*suffering that seems to last forever*." But please hear this: *Longsuffering is **always** associated with <u>hope</u> and <u>mercy</u>*. Therefore, it is the opposite of despair, discouragement and depression. 1 Thessalonians 1:3 confirms this with: "remembering without ceasing your work of faith, labor of love and *<u>patience of hope</u>* [longsuffering] in our Lord Jesus Christ..."

Another definition of longsuffering that I really like is: *believing all things, hoping all things and enduring all things*. Longsuffering here describes someone who *continually* puts all unfulfilled hopes, dreams and visions at the foot of the Cross and <u>never</u> lets go, <u>never</u> gives in and <u>never</u> gives up!

Longsuffering is simply Love that endures all circumstances. Are you willing to learn this kind of Love?

That's what this little book is all about.

Precious Examples

Longsuffering speaks of a person who doesn't give in to dismay, confusion and discouragement when difficult circumstances or trials occur, but patiently endures them without complaint, always "seeing Him who is invisible." (Hebrews 11:27)

First, there's the example of Shadrach, Meshach and Abednego, Daniel's three friends thrown into the fiery furnace, where Nebuchadnezzar had committed them because they would not bow down and worship him. Rather than bemoan their fate, they declared that the "God whom we serve is able to deliver us from the burning fiery furnace, and He will deliver us out of thine hand, O king. But if not, be it known unto thee, O king, that we will not serve thy gods, nor worship the golden image which thou hast set up." (Daniel 3:17-18)

Can you imagine giving this response to the king of the known world at the time? Nebuchadnezzar was so furious at their response that his composure completely changed. He commanded his mighty men to bind the three, make the fire seven times hotter and cast them into it.

We all know the end of the story. When Nebuchadnezzar looked into the fire to see what was happening, he said, "Did we not cast *three* men, bound, into the midst of the fire?" His men answered, "Yes, my Lord." Nebuchadnezzar then said, "I see *four* men loose, **walking in the midst of the fire**, and they have no hurt, and ...the fourth is like the Son of God." (Verses 24-25)

Truly, Shadrach, Meshach and Abednego never let go, never gave in and never gave up! They persevered until they "saw Him who is invisible."

A stunning example of one who hasn't given in to dismay or confusion in her trial but has patiently endured it without complaint, is my dear friend, Christine. Married to a pastor, mother of five children, Christine is desperately trying to hold on to her failing marriage. She has every Biblical right to leave, but more than anything else, she wants the Lord's will. Listen to what she just wrote me:

"Many of us face hardships in our marriages, but *we must never give up on God!* Although the valleys seem dark and it does appear that 'we are troubled on every side, distressed, persecuted and cast down, but in the eyes our faithful God, *we are not distressed, not in despair, not forsaken* and *not destroyed.*' (2 Corinthians 4:8-9) Because we are loved by God and He desires that we live the abundant life. His abundant life only comes from a dying to self and a living for Christ. He is a God that loves to have His children bear fruit. It's not the same fruit that the world bears; that of financial wealth, and material things but the wealth that never rusts and never passes away—the fruit of the spirit. Through the many trials of my life and the one I am currently in, I know that *all* is Father-filtered. He is pruning me and I am beginning to bring forth that precious fruit. The fruit of longsuffering has been the most painful to birth and I have resisted the process many days. But, I am beginning to see the blossom and one day this fruit will be evident for all to see."

The following poem is one that Christine wrote only two weeks ago. She wrote it, as you will hear, from her heart. I know you will agree, after reading it, that God is not only in and all around this beautiful sister in the Lord, but that He has a special future planned out for her. Listen:

> *"As the sun sets each day the night brings despair, somewhere in the darkness my knight has disappeared. The road and the battle have been long and tough, only those in the darkness begin to enjoy the lack of trust.*

> *"The knight that once rode upon a valiant white horse is lost somewhere in the darkness and appears so distraught.*

> *"The one to whom he wed searches for the one that was so true, only to find the shadows of them she once knew.*

> *"Her heart is broken and her head begins to spin, as she feels the enemy approaches, appearing to win.*

> *"The maiden has turned older and a bit worn. Wisdom has crept by, her loved one has gone.*

> *"She sees his shiny armor only in her dreams as she dances there with the man that used to call her queen.*

> *"The younger maiden in the land has caught her husband's eye and the screams you hear are that of a dream that wants to live but only seems to die. The screams are silent many times as she sees him look at her, for that was her valiant knight who has drifted far from her.*

"The old maiden used to feel that love was worth her while and that she would sail off with him and never ever cry.

"Time has past and seasons change, the night won't last forever.   One day the old maiden will awake with hope bound in her heart looking from the past to a brand new start.

"The days grow cold and the screams seem to linger but the maiden knows that it will not always be December.

"The winter will pass and the screams will go away and the maiden will arise with the promise of a new day. As God's promise is bigger than the pain and her latter dreams become true, God's promises will erase the trials and tribulations that caused her disgrace.

"The trials and tribulations will have made her strong and her screams will turn into laughter as the pain turns into song.

"Morning comes alive with the promise of a new day, weeping has turned to joy in a more excellent way. God's Love has overcome and the birds begin to fly, the wind begins to whisper a familiar lullaby, 'Never Give Up' will be the words that the Holy Spirit imparts and that darkness now has turned to day and as the promises embark.

"Longsuffering has blossomed, a new beginning is made, God's promises are certain and this is a new day!!!"

In her letter, Christine went on to write a few thoughts to those experiencing similar trials. This is what she had to say:

"Stay on the vine, the pruning process may make you scream, but the fruit that results is the sweetest in the land. I pray that if you are in the season of pruning that you would allow the fruit of longsuffering to come forth. I pray that in some way this writing will give you a hope of a new tomorrow. God will wipe away all the tears and you will break forth into song. Stronger for the experience, richer in your walk with God. My prayer is that this writing will give you hope. Again, as 2 Corinthians 4:8-9 says, 'We are troubled on every side, *yet not distressed*; we are perplexed, *but not in despair*; persecuted, *but not forsaken*; cast down, *but not destroyed.*'"

This book is chock-full of examples like Christine. Men and women who in spite of their horrific circumstances, have chosen to never let go, never give in and *never give up.* We'll explore their situations and learn just "how" they are able to do it.

Never giving up is what this little book is all about. *How do we avoid becoming overwhelmed and dismayed at our horrifying and tragic trials? How do we persevere through them rather than falling apart in them?* And, *how do we take a negative situation (in our minds) and turn it around into a positive one?* Remember, Isaiah 41:10: "**Be not dismayed, for I am your God. I will strengthen you; I will help you. I will uphold you...**" Again, this is our promise. This is our commission. And this is our hope!

But, first, we must learn to do our part in that promise: not to become dismayed; ***never to give up!***

In light of this, Hebrews 6:12 is an interesting Scripture. It tells us that we are to be followers of them who through *faith* and *patience* (i.e., longsuffering) inherit the promises of God. Well, let me ask you a question: Could the reverse also be true? *If we don't learn longsuffering, we won't inherit God's promises.* Wow! Read that again! Could this Scripture be telling us that only as we learn patiently to endure will the Lord's promises be fulfilled in our lives? It's just a question, but it certainly tells me that longsuffering is an essential "fruit" and that it <u>must</u> be learned in order to embrace all of God's promises.

Definition of Suffering

The definition for the word "suffering" is probably quite different from what you might imagine. Suffering means "barring our selves from following sin and self." In other words, when we choose to bar ourselves from following what *we* want, what *we* feel and what *we* desire, and choose, instead, to follow what *Jesus* has asked, we often do suffer. It's hard to say "no" to self and "yes" to God. And, it's difficult to put another's interests and needs before our own.

"L o n g" suffering then, is simply a means of un-selfing us. As someone said to me yesterday, it's the means by which we *unlearn* all that we have learned so far by the flesh; and, it's a *relearning* of everything all over again by the Spirit. This in-between learning time is often called "longsuffering."

The root of the word "longsuffering" in the Greek is *thumos* which means anger, wrath or indignation. Longsuffering means "holding back or restraining" what we really feel (anger, wrath or indignation) and what we really want to do; and instead, doing what God wants us to do. The way we hold back or restrain our natural response is by choosing to give our anger, wrath and bitterness, etc., to God, rather than acting upon them. Again, it's "barring ourselves from following what we would really like to do" and, instead, doing what God wants us to do. God, then, promises to be our champion, our defender and our vindicator.

When we learn to respond in this way, Romans 5:3-5 tells us we'll be able to "glory in [our] tribulations...knowing that tribulation worketh patience; and patience, *experience*; and experience, *hope*; and, hope maketh not ashamed, because the *Love of God* is shed abroad in our hearts by the Holy Spirit which is given to us."

Note, by the way, the order of spiritual growth here: <u>hope</u> and <u>love</u> are apprehended only *after* <u>patient enduring</u> and <u>experience</u>. Not *before*!

An Extreme Example

An extreme example of this is the life of Dietrich Bonhoeffer, a pastor, professor and one of the most brilliant minds of the twentieth century. He witnessed Adolf Hitler's diabolical rise to power in the 1930's. After struggling with the moral issues involved, he joined the resistance movement. He was found out, caught and put into solitary confinement until they hanged him just a few weeks before World War II ended. He wrote a magnificent work called *The Cost of Discipleship* and paid the cost with his life. It is a classic today.

A biography of Bonhoeffer's life describes him as never truly being alone because, as the author puts it, "the Lord was always with him." Anchoring his daily life in the simple disciplines of Bible study and prayer, he used his time in prison to ponder and write on deep spiritual issues.[1]

We will be quoting Bonhoeffer quite often throughout this book. He felt strongly that *"fulfilment of the Christian life can only be found on the other side of suffering."* Only patient enduring and experience can bring about the hope and love we are all seeking.

The End Times

I truly believe we are living in the "end times," because something drastic has changed in the world. Something has been unleashed. Something is different!

David Wilkerson in his *Times Square Pulpit Series* (June, 2003 & Sept. 2004 issues) wrote:

> "In all my years of ministry, I've never seen so many believers under such affliction. There has never been a time like this, with families facing financial crises, enduring marital struggles, despairing over children in rebellion...Wives and families are being overwhelmed. Pastors are quitting by the hundreds in every nation...Everywhere we go, we see pandemic despair..."

> "We're living in a time of the greatest gospel revelation in history. There are more preachers, more books, and more gospel-media saturation than ever. *Yet there has never been more distress, affliction and troubled minds among God's people.*"

From my own walk of 47 years with the Lord, it appears that God has begun to wrap up life as we know it. He's accomplishing this by allowing more world problems, a greater magnitude of personal problems and a wave of evil that we have not experienced before. Consequently, Christians are being forced to choose sides. The Lord is not letting us be "fence sitters" any more. Lukewarmness is no longer to be tolerated. In these end times, no one is exempt from God's purging. We're all in the "fire" together. Thus, rather than get burned up from ignorance, apathy and fear, let's find out how to use our difficult times *to* our advantage and *for* His glory.

1 Peter 4:17 reminds us that "the time is come that judgment must begin at the house of God." Now, I never thought I would live long enough to see this Scripture come alive before my very eyes. But, it has! It's telling us that each of us, every Christian, will pass under the judgment of God. Every aspect of our lives will be tested; all our secrets exposed; all our motives revealed. The method God uses to accomplish this will come through our tribulations. It has been aptly said that we are forged in the crucible of adversity!

James 1:3-4 teaches that "the testing of [our] faith produces patience. But [we are to] let patience have its perfect work, that [we] may be *perfect and complete*, lacking nothing." Clearly, it is the fruit of longsuffering that transforms us into the image of Christ. Wow!

These are heavy Scriptures.

So, no matter how we look at it, "longsuffering" seems to go with being a Christian, certainly nowadays. Most of us probably didn't realize this when we "signed on." But at this point in our walk with the Lord, *we have no other choice but to proceed.* Luke reminds us that those who look back are not fit for the kingdom. (Luke 9:62) Besides, where else would we go? Who else has the answers to life? And who else knows the end from the beginning? Only Jesus Christ.

God wants us to glorify (reflect) Him in every situation, no matter how difficult. In doing so, we prove that we do, indeed, love Him. In Genesis 22:12, the Lord says to Abraham, who in obedience would have sacrificed his only son, that now He knows "that you fear [love] God, seeing that you have not withheld thy son [your most precious possession]..." We, too, must learn how to love the Lord in all circumstances, not withholding *our most precious possessions—our dreams, our hopes and our visions*—but willingly laying them down at the Cross, remembering that nothing can touch us but what God has not *first* ordained. In other words, no person, no situation, no tragedy and no illness can come into our lives that is not "Father filtered"—allowed by His sovereign permission. And when He does say "yes" to certain situations, He promises to 'be with us, not fail or forsake us, to strengthen us, help us and uphold us.'

The most wonderful promise of all is 2 Timothy 2:12, "If we suffer [deny self], *we shall also reign with Him.*" Could the reverse also be true?

I believe the Lord is telling us here that the fruit of longsuffering is absolutely critical to experience, imperative to implement and essential to display. There seem to be eternal consequences!

What About Us?

Most of us talk very openly about "being like Christ" and of having His characteristics of Love, joy, peace, etc., but what about the fruit of longsuffering—that determination to *never give up*? Do we also manifest this fruit to others? How easy it is for us simply to *preach* "Christ crucified" without ever really living it.[2] One of Jesus' main characteristics was longsuffering Love! So the question we must constantly ask ourselves is, how can we preach Christ crucified if we really don't understand what longsuffering is all about?

Someone made a statement to me recently that was absolutely profound: she said, "It's crucial that the messenger becomes the message itself." Think about that for a moment. The messenger (the one relaying God's Word) must become the message (one living God's Word). What she was saying is that we must not only "talk the talk," we must also "live" the message of God's Love, joy, peace and longsuffering.

How can we even talk about the fruit of the Spirit, if we don't manifest all of it? There's no way we can communicate God's message of Love to others, especially in trials, if we have not first experienced it for ourselves! Head knowledge can only produce head knowledge in others. Heart knowledge can only produce heart knowledge. But, "foot knowledge" (His life showing forth in our actions) births "foot knowledge" in others.

Our daily prayer should be exactly what Paul prayed in 2 Corinthians 4:12, that death [of self] would work in us, so that Christ's life could be formed in others.

Longsuffering is God's means of answering that prayer.

Yet, the question remains: how do we *do* it?

"Though He slay me, yet will I *trust* Him."
(Job 13:15)

Chapter 1
God's Cycle of Trust

Why Trials and Suffering?

Trials, problems and tragedies come to <u>all</u> Christians. They come because of personal sin, they come because of the sins of others, they come because of the schemes of the devil, and they come because God has allowed them for our growth. In my book *Faith in the Night Seasons* we covered some of the basic reasons why God allows trials.

1) To strengthen our faith and trust in Him
    (1 Peter 5:10)

2) To produce all the fruit of the Spirit
    (Hebrews 10:36; James 1:3; Psalm 30:5)

3) To silence the enemy (Job 1:9-12; 2:3-7)

4) To glorify Himself through us (John 9:1-3;
    11:1-4)

5) To conform us more into His image
    (Philippians 3:10)

6) To enlarge our ministry (2 Corinthians 1:3-7)

7) So that we might see, and then deal, with our
    sin (1 Peter 2:20; Hebrews 12:5-9)

8) And, finally, to search our hearts to see if we
    really love Him (as in Genesis 22)

Judges 2:20-23 is a perfect example of this last point. In this chapter God tests the Israelites by *not* driving out their enemy, but, instead, letting their enemy stand and not be conquered. How many of us have experienced a similar time when God *doesn't* seem to answer our prayers, but actually allows the opposite to occur! This Scripture tells us that He does so simply to know our hearts and to see if we love Him.

A precious, single Christian woman I know just recently experienced this very thing. She moved away from her home, her job and her family because of a very painful experience. She was convinced that God had told her to move and that He would bless her in the new situation.

But, unfortunately, once she settled in the new city, got a great job and a wonderful apartment, all hell broke loose. Her friends betrayed her, her job evaporated, a relationship she prayed would work out disintegrated; and now she's wondering if she ever heard God at all.

The Lord is obviously very concerned with our comfort, our security and our future, but I believe He is primarily concerned with how those circumstances are going to affect us internally. In other words, will they bring about a changed heart and a transformed life? In the long run, will they draw us closer to Him? And will they cause us to love others more? Again, as someone said to me recently, God's more interested with the sanctification process *in us*, than He is with the success or the attainment that we are after. Remember, God's ways are opposite to the world's ways. Now that's not exactly what we want to hear, but I do believe it's the truth.

God's ways are not our ways. He's not interested in the "outward" man. He looks at our hearts, our true motives and our real intents. This is what He wants exposed. Not for His own benefit, for He already knows the truth, but for our own. He wants *us* to see it for ourselves.

The woman above is slowly beginning to realize all of this as she looks back over the last year of her life and sees God's handiwork. *Hind-sight is wonderful, isn't it?*

One of our natural responses in a trial, however, is to blame the enemy for most everything that happens. In reality, however, we must acknowledge that <u>not</u> every difficult situation comes from him. Please don't misunderstand me, the enemy is *always* involved when difficult things occur in our lives and he rejoices when we get into trouble or when we react poorly to what the Lord has allowed. Our negative reactions give him more ammunition and more inroads into our soul. But the enemy, himself, is <u>not</u> always the one responsible for sending the trial. God often does that! This is a hard truth to hear; but listen to what Isaiah 53:10 has to say, in speaking about Jesus, "Yet it pleased the Lord to bruise Him;... [and] put Him to grief."

I believe there are times that God must do the same with us. What the Lord means to use "for good" in our lives, the enemy, on the other hand is right there trying to use to destroy.

How We Respond is Key

In all of this, the most important thing is "how we respond." Whether we withdraw, advance or simply stay where we are, which is really impossible, depends upon our moment-by-moment responses. Because <u>this</u>

is what will determine our whole spiritual future. If we understand what <u>God</u> wants from us and what <u>we</u> are to do, then we can remain peaceful in the eye of the storm and come through the circumstances quickly. If, however, we don't understand what God is after and we react poorly to His set-up, then we'll stumble, become confused and only prolong our agony.

Some tragic examples of this are:

After losing his job, his home and his family, Mike (a dear, Christian friend of mine) commented, "Nancy, where's God in all of this? I feel completely abandoned. And, I just can't take it anymore. I'm giving up. I'm out of here."

This response broke my heart.

Another Christian woman cried out in a recent counseling session, "What have I done to deserve all of this? Praying doesn't seem to help. Reading the Word is useless. I'm going back to what I know."

I could hardly hold back my tears.

And, finally, another brother asked, "What about all God's promises to me? How could He allow this to happen? I can't trust Him anymore! I'm just going to have to get myself out of this mess."

No, no, no! The answer is <u>not</u> to give up, *but to trust more!*

All the above responses are disastrous. And their emotional outburst cost them in their relationship with the Lord. It severed their communication with Him and quenched His Spirit at the time that they needed Him the most.

When God's promise seems to fail and the vision tarry, it's <u>not</u> time to grow weary and give up, even though that's exactly what we "feel" like doing. *It's a time to do just the opposite! It's a time to hang on tighter, trust the Lord further and **never give up**!*

Remember, in Exodus 32, where all the Israelites in the wilderness "gave up" on Moses on the mount and began making for themselves a golden calf? And remember, too, in Numbers 13, where all but two of the spies *gave up* because, they said, giants "dwell in the land...and they are stronger than we."

Again, we must remind ourselves in our crises that it's not a time to grow weary and give up, but a time to trust the Lord further and *never give up*. A time to say, "Though He slay me, yet will I trust Him." (Job 13:15)

So, how should the above Christians have responded? What should they have done? What steps would have made their circumstances more tolerable? How could they have had victory in their storms?

Jesus is Our Example

We are told throughout the New Testament to keep our eyes upon Jesus because *He is our example*. He showed us how to think, how to act, how to live and how to respond. The apostle Peter validates this in 1 Peter 2:21:

> "For even hereunto were ye called, because Christ also suffered for us, *leaving us an example, that ye should follow His steps*."[3]

Also in 1 Peter 4:1:

> "Forasmuch, then, as Christ hath suffered
> for us in the flesh, *arm yourselves likewise*
> *with the same mind* [or the same attitude]."

Jesus is not only our Savior, our Lord and our
King, He is also our role model, our standard and our
example. Jesus defined the Christian life for us. He
walked it "perfectly." He showed us how it's supposed
to be done, how it's supposed to be walked and how
it's supposed to be lived. Now, obviously, we'll *never*
be able to emulate Jesus perfectly, but Scripture tells us
that we are to set Him as our example. We are to learn
by His model. In other words, if God used the "way
of suffering" in Jesus' life to accomplish His will, then
it's reasonable to expect that *He will use our trials and*
our suffering to accomplish His will in our lives also.

Bonhoeffer wrote, "The cross means sharing the
suffering of Christ to the last and to the fullest... If we
refuse to take up our cross and submit to suffering and
rejection at the hands of men, we forfeit our fellowship
with Christ and have ceased to follow Him..." And,
again, there is "no easy way to God, for He resides
behind the Cross."[4]

2 Peter 3:15 teaches that it was only through "the
longsuffering of Jesus" that <u>we</u> received salvation!
Take a minute to comprehend what this Scripture is
saying. If the Lord arranged for us to be saved *only*
through His longsuffering—through His patiently
enduring our failures, our blunders and our errors, are
we not to do the same for our families, our friends and
our loved ones? Perhaps *our* longsuffering towards
other people might eventually bring them salvation—
just as Jesus' did for us.

Love That Endures

Matthew 24:12 is a Scripture that I have quoted many, many times over the past 25 years in regards to the *Way of Agape*: "And because iniquity shall abound, *the Love [Agape] of many shall grow cold.*" But, take a look at the very next verse in regards to *longsuffering or never giving up*: "he that shall endure unto the end, the same shall be saved."

The word "endure" here is *hupomeno* which means to stay under or to stay behind. Endurance is the agency by which we stay, abide, continue in, and dwell under. Just as Jesus endured the Cross, we, too, must stay under, courageously suffering and enduring all the difficult situations that the Lord allows in our lives. Why? So that others may come to know Christ through our patient hope and loving endurance.

Hupomeno can also mean "perseverance." Perseverance is far more than simple endurance. And, it's far more than just hanging on. Perseverance means *continuing* to fight, *continuing* to act and *continuing* to initiate. I am reminded of Jashobeam, the chief captain of David's army, who slew 300 foes at one time with only his spear. (1 Chronicles 11)

Perseverance is endurance combined with absolute assurance and certainty that what we are looking for, will happen. Again, it's ***never giving up!***

Listen to some of the incredible Scriptural promises to those Christians who persevere, endure and never give up:

Mark 13:13, "...*he that shall <u>endure</u> unto the end, the same shall be saved.*" ("saved")

2 Timothy 2:10, "Therefore, I <u>endure</u> all things for the elects' sake, *that they may also obtain the salvation* which is in Christ Jesus with eternal glory." ("salvation")

Hebrews 12:7, "If ye <u>endure</u> chastening, God dealeth with you as with sons; for what son is he whom the father chasteneth not?" ("sonship")

Revelation 3:10, "Because [you] have kept the word of my patience [*hupomeno*], *I also will keep [you] from the hour of temptation,* which shall come upon all the world to try them." ("kept from coming evil times")

James 5:11, "Behold, we count them happy who <u>endure</u>. Ye have heard of the *patience of Job, and have seen the end of the Lord,* that the Lord is very pitiful and of tender mercy." ("mercy of the Lord")

1 Corinthians 13:4 & 7, "Love...beareth all things, believeth all things, hopeth all things, *<u>endureth </u>all things*." ("never failing Love")

James 1:12, "*Blessed is the man that <u>endureth</u> temptation;* for when he is tried, he shall receive the crown of life, which the Lord hath promised to them that love Him." ("crown of life")

Notice in all of the above Scriptures what one who *never gives up* receives: salvation, sonship, protection from tribulation, the mercy of the Lord, unfailing Love and the crown of life. *Aren't these worth learning the fruit of longsuffering?* You decide...

God uses our trials and our suffering to accomplish His highest will and purposes in our lives. 1 Peter 5:10 assures us that "after you have suffered awhile," the God of all grace will "perfect, establish, strengthen, and settle you."

Because our trials can come upon us suddenly and without advance warning, they can end up in either one of two ways: **cycle of trust** or **cycle of defeat**. If we know what God's basic will is and we trust Him, then we can, at least, have the faith that no matter what <u>we</u> see or feel, He will work out His perfect will in our lives in His timing and way.

What is God's Will?

This brings up a very good question: What exactly is God's *basic* will for our lives? It's easy to say that God will use our trials and our suffering to accomplish His will in our lives, but what exactly does this mean?

God's will *for all mankind* is that we might have a personal and eternal relationship with Him through salvation. As John 3:13-17 says, Christ came so that <u>all</u> might be saved. God's will *for believers*, however, is much more specific. He wants <u>all</u> Christians *to be conformed into His image by the process of sanctification.* (Romans 8:29; 1 Thessalonians 5:23; Hebrews 6:1) In brief, He wants to reproduce His Life in us, including the fruit of longsuffering which, as we said, was one of Jesus' most precious characteristics. (John 10:10a)

I have always taught that God's basic will for our lives is that we be conformed into Christ's image, but for some reason I never realized the full ramifications of this statement. Not only does God want us to be conformed into His image of Love, joy, peace, etc., *but also to be conformed into His image of endurance, longsuffering, forbearing and perseverance.* This is what the process of sanctification is all about—teaching us how to never let go, never give in and ***never give up,*** no matter what the cost. It cost Jesus *everything.* He gave up His heavenly place of authority and humbled Himself to take on humanity. He gave to us in a complete outpouring of His Godhood, of sacrifice for us, and perhaps He risked beyond what we can even imagine. Are we willing to do the same for Him?

Again, Bonhoeffer relates: "The wondrous theme of the Bible that frightens so many people is that the only visible sign of God in the world is the cross. Christ is not carried away from earth to heaven in glory, but He must go to the cross. And precisely there, where the cross stands, the resurrection is near; even there, where everyone begins to doubt God, where everyone despairs of God's power, there God is whole, there Christ is active and near. Where the power of darkness does violence to the light of God, there God triumphs and judges the darkness."[5]

Trusting God Is Essential

The first place we must begin our exploration of the fruit of longsuffering—never giving up—is with the concept of trusting God. The only way we can ever learn this most precious characteristic of His, is by unconditionally trusting Him.

What exactly is trust? The Greek word is *peitho* which means "to rely upon, to have confidence in or to believe in." Think about it for moment. Trust encompasses absolutely everything. Everything we think, say and do is built upon either trust in *someone* or trust in *something.* Most of us have learned the hard way that if we put our trust in material things or other people, we'll usually be let down. That leaves us with just two other options: either put our trust in ourselves, which again most of us have found out to be deadly (see Proverbs 28:26), or put our trust in the Lord. We *cannot* do both. We cannot fully trust in God and trust in ourselves at the same time. We must choose one or the other.

For Christians, Hebrews 2:13 tells us that there is only one correct answer. We must unconditionally trust in the Lord and Him alone. He is the <u>only</u> One who has all the answers to life. He is the only One who knows all the intricate plans He has for our individual lives. And He is the only One who can control what comes in and out of our lives. *Trusting God means cleaving to Him with unreserved confidence no matter how we feel, what we see or what we understand; being fully persuaded that what He has promised, He <u>will</u> perform in His timing and in His way.* (Romans 4:20)

By experience, most of us have learned that God's ways are often far far beyond our human understanding. Thus, if we are to walk with Him, love Him and experience His Life through us, we must unreservedly cling to the assurance that whatever He allows in our lives is <u>for a purpose</u>. *Being able to trust Him, rely upon Him and have confidence in Him in these times is absolutely essential.* If we give in to doubting His Love and His care at this time, we can easily lose our way. It's impossible to do His will and learn longsuffering without being able to trust Him completely!

The Lord's *Cycle of Trust*

One of my favorite Scriptures is Psalm 37:5 which says: "Commit your way unto the Lord; trust also in Him; and He will bring it to pass." Trusting God is simply <u>knowing</u> and being absolutely assured that *He will do <u>all</u> He promises.* Remember the definition of perseverance—*certainty that what we are looking for, will happen.* Trusting God is the basis of that perseverance.

Trust incorporates many things,—from knowing what His will is to walking it out. And, of course, it incorporates the whole process in between. The more we understand what trust really is, the more we'll be able to confidently walk out His will. Like many other principles in the Christian life, trust doesn't just happen; *it's a learned experience.* Simply *saying* "Though He slay me, yet will I trust Him" is far different than actually *living out* being slain and still trusting Him. Trust begins with *one faith choice* at a time. When we experience God's faithfulness in the first incident, we'll have the confidence to make the same kind of choice in all the rest.

There are eight principles that make up God's **cycle of trust.** These eight principles (each of which makes up some form or aspect of trusting Him) will take us from beginning knowledge of God to intimate knowledge of Him. These are principles that you and I have bantered around for years and thought we understood. But perhaps we'll see, for the first time, how these terms are interrelated. They not only depend upon each other but also build upon each other. Consequently, unless we are "living" the first principle, we'll be unable to go on to the next. And if we are not living that one, the third one will be out of our reach. And so on. All these principles are related and must go in the order God has laid them out. Again, *each defines some aspect of trusting God.*

So, after 47 years of being a Christian and many, many stumbles and falls, this is what I see as the Lord's **cycle of trust**: (You check me out. We have the same Guide Book.)

1) First, we must **know His basic will.** We must know what He desires to do in our lives. Romans 8:29 tells us He wants to "conform us into His image."

2) Next, we must **know He unconditionally loves us**. We must know this not just in our heads but in our everyday experience.

3) As a result of the above two things, we'll be able to trust Him enough **to obey Him** by faith, not feelings

The way we obey Him is:

4) Choosing to **love Him**— continually giving our selves over to Him.

5) Choosing to **renew our Mind**—continually dealing with our sin and self.

6) Choosing to **have absolute faith**—continually walking by faith, not feelings.

7) If we are doing the above, we'll have the ability to **see Him in all things**.

8) And, as a result of this, we'll be able to **patiently endure all He has allowed**.

In simpler terms, knowing **His Love** produces **our obedience** which brings about **His presence** and the ability **to persevere** through any trial.

These are the principles that make up the Lord's **cycle of trust** and leaving any one of them out puts a hole in our ability to trust Him fully. Each principle depends completely upon our living the previous one. Leaving out one of the precepts will prevent us from going on to the next one. For example: there's no way we can love God, (lay our wills and our lives down before Him) unless we *first* know that He loves us.

So the bottom line is: we can only learn the fruit of longsuffering by living all eight of God's principles

of trust, His **cycle of trust**. If we fall down in any of
these steps of trust, chances are we'll feel like giving
up, letting go and turning back. And, most likely,
we'll not survive our crises without confusion and
devastation.

Interestingly, this **cycle of trust** is a chronology
of my own walk with the Lord. First, I learned about
His Love and what His will was (when my marriage
fell apart). Then, He proceeded to teach me what
He desired from me (obedience): how to love Him,
how to renew my mind and how to have naked faith
(throughout desperate circumstances in my own life—
as I will share later). As a result of applying these
principles to my life, I began to see Him as I never
had before. So, again, **His Love** in my life produced a
willingness to obey Him in all things, which resulted
in my **seeing Him** and being able to **endure** through
harsh and tragic circumstances.

Even for us older Christians, trusting the Lord
completely during horrific trials and tragedies is
still hard. The route our natural minds take when
everything falls apart in our lives is *not* towards
trusting, enduring and persevering, but towards
discouragement, confusion and depression. Being
willing unconditionally to trust the Lord and *not lean
to our own understanding* is essential. (Proverbs 3:5)

Only *living* God's **cycle of trust** will allow us
to say, "Though You slay me, yet will I trust You..."
(Job 13:15)

Personal Example: Chip

Here's a personal example:

Five years ago, when I was in the middle of
writing the book *Faith in the Night Seasons*, God

allowed one of the biggest trials of my trust in Him ever,—probably the hardest thing I will ever have to face. One Saturday night as we all sat around the dining room table eating dinner, came the unthinkable phone call: "We are very sorry to inform you that your son, Chip, has just died."

Our beloved "Chip," our firstborn son, Charles Jr., had suddenly died of a massive heart attack while out jogging. He was only 39 years old, married with two precious little girls, 3 years old and 6 months old. Chip had not seen a doctor for five years. He had been in excellent health and had no prior medical problems. He had run for fun and pleasure all his life, from high school races to recent city-wide events. He had personally known the Lord for about 20 years and had just recently re-committed his life.

There is no reason on earth why this tragedy should have happened. There is no human understanding for it and we could spend years trying to figure out "why" God allowed it. The fact is that He did, and only He understands the full ramifications of "why." Chuck and I have chosen, by faith, to leave all our questions at the Cross, and implicitly trust God in it.

This is where faith choices fit in. Faith choices are choices we make by faith, not feelings. God, then, in His timing and in His way aligns our feelings with the Godly choices we have made. We'll talk more about faith choices as we go, but that first year after Chip's death, I probably chose, by faith, a hundred times a day, "to give the situation back to God" and unconditionally trust Him in it. I certainly didn't feel like making those choices, but I did it out of obedience. And God was faithful to eventually align my feelings with my faith choices.

Blessings Resulting From Sorrows

Through Chip's death, I've learned that *trusting God is simply accepting a situation I cannot fully understand and no longer being troubled by it.* Because God has taught me His **cycle of trust**, I know by faith that *there is no sorrow so great that He cannot somehow "recycle" it to bring forth a blessing.* And this is exactly what He has done with Chip's passing.

The first blessing we were able to see as a direct result of his death was that my 86-year-old Christian Science mom, my daughter-in-law and my grandson all came to know Christ personally. Another blessing was that my other son, Mark, came fully back to the Lord. And, finally, mom's 96-year-old "boyfriend," Doug, accepted Christ as a result of seeing the change in Mom's life. Both she and Doug have since passed on. But, the biggest blessing for us is that we now know exactly where they are—at peace with Chip and waiting for us to join them. These are all miracles that Chip would have willingly given his life for. And, in a sense, he did!

So, it's true, there is no sorrow so great that God cannot somehow use it to bring forth a blessing. If we are living God's **cycle of trust,** we'll be able to recognize the blessings when they come, because we'll be expecting them. If, however, we are unable to live God's **cycle of trust** for whatever reason, we'll find ourselves on a path towards doubt and unbelief.

Only Two Choices in the Eye of the Storm

Because trials often come upon us suddenly, they can produce either of two results: 1) We can be left with *more* trust and faith in the Lord, or 2) We can be consumed with doubt and disbelief in His care and love. Many of us have experienced both.

If we know what God's basic will is for our lives (to form Christ's character in us) and we unconditionally trust Him to do so, *then* we'll be able to experience a "peace that passes all understanding," even in the midst of our trials. If, however, we are confused about what God is doing in our lives and we *don't* trust Him (we're not living His **cycle of trust**), then we'll experience doubt that He is even there, unbelief that He cares and, eventually, a hardness of heart and a falling away from the faith.

Doubt is the first step towards that defeat.

Nothing will bring us down faster than doubt, because it affects every choice we make. Doubt in God's faithfulness and Love will influence everything we do. Everything we think, say and do is either impacted by our faith in the Lord or by our doubt in His existence. Doubt robs us of our vision, immobilizes our actions and defeats our even trying. It also thwarts every effort we might want to make in the future! Doubt can easily spiral out of control and lead us to discouragement, which then breeds confusion and results in depression. This is the enemy's formula for defeat—his **cycle of defeat**! *Doubt—discouragement—confusion—depression—loss of vision—disorientation—despair and defeat.* The feeling of "giving up." And, oh, how many of us have fallen for it!

See Chart on page 45

Doubt can be traced back to unbelief in God's Word and His promises. His Word is our *fixed point of reference*. His Word is infallible. (John 8:44) But it happens that when a person's trust in God is shaken, faith in His Word also wavers. At such a point, we must not only guard against the enemy inserting doubt into our minds about God's faithfulness, but we must also be careful that he doesn't twist Scripture, which can lead us to uncertainty—especially when things don't turn out as we hoped. The enemy not only wants to insert doubt and twist Scripture, he also wants to attack us with the Word. We must be ready for these assaults, ready to defend God and His Word at all costs. And the way we do that is by continually saying by faith, "Though [You] slay me, yet *I will [choose to] trust You.*" (Job 13:15)

When God's promise seems to fail and His vision tarry, it's not a time to grow weary and give up but, rather *a time to trust Him even more*.

An Example: Aggie

Here's a story that graphically shows one man's slide down the enemy's **cycle of defeat**. All because, he doubted... This story is from one of David Wilkerson's newsletters.[6]

"In 1921, two young missionary couples in Stockholm, Sweden, received a burden to go to the Belgian Congo (which is now Zaire). David and Svea Flood (along with their 2-year old son) joined Joel and Bertha Erickson to battle insects, fierce heat, malaria and malnutrition. But after six months in the jungle, they had made little or no contact with the native people. Although the Erickson's decided to return to the mission station, the Floods chose to stay in their lonely outpost. Svea was now pregnant and sick with malaria, yet she faithfully continued to minister to their one and only convert, a little boy from one of the nearby villages.

"Svea died after giving birth to a healthy baby girl, and as David Flood stood over his beloved wife's grave, he poured out his bitterness to God: 'Why did You allow this?

(**doubt**) We came here to give our lives, and now my wife is dead at 27! All we have to show for all this is one little village boy who probably doesn't even understand what we've told him. You've failed me, God. What a waste of life!' (**discouragement and confusion**)

"David Flood ended up leaving his new daughter with the Erickson's and taking his son back home with him to Sweden. He then went into the import business, and never allowed the name of 'God' to be mentioned in his presence. (**loss of vision and disorientation**) His little girl was raised in the Congo by an American missionary couple, who named their adopted daughter 'Aggie.'

"Throughout her life, Aggie tried to locate her real father, but her letters were never answered. She never knew that David Flood had remarried and fathered four more children, and she never knew that he had plunged into despair and had become a total alcoholic. But when she was in her forties, Aggie and her husband were given round-trip tickets to Sweden, and while spending a day's layover in London, the couple went to hear a well-known black preacher from the Belgian Congo.

"After the meeting, Aggie asked the preacher, 'Did you ever know David and Svea Flood?' To her great surprise, he answered, 'Svea Flood led me to the Lord when I was a little boy.' Aggie was ecstatic to learn that her mother's only convert was being mightily used to evangelize Zaire, and he was overjoyed to meet the daughter of the woman who had introduced him to Christ.

"When Aggie arrived in Sweden, she located her father in an impoverished area of Stockholm, living in a rundown apartment filled with empty liquor bottles. (**despair and darkness**) David Flood was now a 73-year old diabetic who had had a stroke and whose eyes were covered with cataracts, yet when she identified herself, he began to weep and apologize for abandoning her. But when Aggie said, 'That's okay, Daddy. God took care of me,' he became totally enraged.

"'God didn't take care of you!' he cried. 'He ruined our whole family! He led us to Africa and then betrayed us! Nothing ever came of our time there, and it was a waste of our lives!' (**defeat**)

"That's when Aggie told him about the black preacher she'd just met in London, and how the Congo had been evangelized through the efforts of his wife's one and only convert. As he listened to his daughter, the Holy Spirit suddenly fell on David Flood, and tears of sorrow and repentance began to flow down his face. Although God mercifully restored him before he died, David Flood left behind five unsaved and embittered children. *His anger towards God had totally wasted his life's potential, and created a tragic legacy for his family.*" (**giving up**)

This story clearly illustrates the fact that we must *never* doubt God or base our faith upon our own human understanding of what God is doing. Had David Flood chosen by an act of his will to accept his situation as coming directly from the hand of God, who knows what awesome fruit God could have brought forth from his life? Only faith will allow us to unabashedly accept His promises, even though we cannot see or understand how they will ever come about.

Choosing to Believe

As seen in the above story, doubting the character of God will immediately stop our spiritual growth, devour our faith and set us on the enemy's **cycle of defeat**. *The only way we can ever counteract doubt, is by an act of our will—i.e., by choosing to believe by faith (not feelings) that no matter what happens, God will never deceive us, never let us down and never abandon us.*

We must submit ourselves to the trial that God has allowed, accept what is happening and allow the Holy Spirit to resolve it for us. *We must love God without the need to see or understand exactly what He is doing.* God is involved in every aspect of our existence and there is no sorrow so great that He cannot somehow "recycle" it to bring forth blessing—as seen in our Chip's passing.

Only our unconditional trust will allow us to unabashedly *accept His promises, even though we cannot see or understand how they will ever come about.* This is expressed and shown beautifully in the life of Abraham whom God had promised an heir, and who "against hope believed in hope" (Romans 4:18-21) and also in Hebrews 11, which lists the saints, who "all died in faith, not having received the promises, but having seen them afar off, and were persuaded of them, and embraced them."

Thus, *the triumph of faith is seen just as much in the bearing of a temporary defeat as it is in the securing of a victory.* Read that again! We grow even more in faith when we experience a set-back, than we do when we have a mountain-top encounter. God wants to conform us into His whole image, and does so through trials, tribulations and tragedies. Overcomers are simply those who, regardless of how they feel or what is going on in their lives, are ready to die rather than give up trusting God.

In conclusion, some important points to remember when we are going through suffering, are:

- God allows troubles in our lives to drive us to our knees and to bring us back to Himself.[7]
- Sometimes our troubles must get worse before freedom comes.
- We must realize that <u>we</u> can't get ourselves out of trouble. If God has allowed the trial, then <u>He</u> will be the only One who can get us out. Remember, the battle is not ours, but His.[8]
- Our troubles should always push us towards God, not away from Him.[9] If they push us away from Him, we should check to see who is the instigator.[10]
- Once we understand that God is involved in our trial, it should give us hope.[11]
- God wants to use our trials to help us learn His statutes and His laws.[12]

God always has a reason for the things He allows in our lives. He is preparing us for a future which He alone knows. He is preparing us as His "bride." He not only wants to make us perfect (holy), established, strengthened and grounded in Him, but also joint heirs.[13]

"Though You slay me, yet will I [choose] to trust You." (Job 13:15)

In the Eye of the Storm
Two Choices

The Lord's *Cycle of Trust*	The Enemy's *Cycle of Defeat*

Knowing His will (faith in His plan for our lives)

↓

Knowing God loves us in spite of what has occurred in our lives

↓

Obediently choosing to do His will

↓

Loving Him—laying our s wills and lives down to Him

↓

Constantly renewing our minds

↓

Walking by faith, not feelings

↓

Seeing Him in all things

↓

Persevering—no matter what the circumstances

↓

NEVER GIVE UP

Doubting God's plan for our lives

↓

Discouragement over what has occurred—God doesn't love me

↓

Confusion over what His will is

↓

Depression—holding tight to our own wills and lives

↓

Complete loss of vision

↓

Disorientation—emotions out of control

↓

Despair and darkness

↓

Total defeat

↓

GIVE UP AND DIE

"We love Him, because He first loved us."
(1 John 4:19)

Chapter 2
Experiencing God's Love

So, the first principle in the Lord's **cycle of trust** is knowing His will: knowing that we are to be conformed into His image. However, we will not be able to do this unless we *first* know that He loves us. Simply put, we cannot lay our wills and our lives down to someone (even God), if we're not assured of that one's love for us. Let me explain:

Years ago, when I first began teaching *The Way of Agape*, I focused on the first two commandments. "Thou shalt love the Lord, thy God, with all thy heart, and with all thy soul, and with all thy mind...and thou shalt love thy neighbour as thyself." (Matthew 22:37-39)

After several years of seeing the reactions of the women in those first classes, I realized there was no way they could ever learn to love God with all their heart, soul and mind *until they first knew that He loved them*. In other words, even if they intellectually knew that He loved them, they could not trust Him unconditionally until they knew that He personally and experientially, loved them. Thus it's imperative that we know God loves us *before* we can lay down our wills and our lives to Him. Consequently, *knowing that God loves us is crucial to our faith*. Without personally "experiencing" His Love and acceptance, we won't be able to move forward in our Christian walk.

Therefore, *before* we can learn to obey God, we need to know without a doubt that He loves us. If we know this, then we'll have the confidence and the trust to unconditionally surrender ourselves to Him.

Knowing God loves us is our foundation, our building pad and the solid rock upon which our whole spiritual house must be built. Only then, will we be able to unilaterally trust and obey God, no matter how difficult our situations become or how hard they are to endure. Once we know He loves us, then we can move forward and respond to our trials the way He desires.

The Bible tells us that, "We love Him, [simply] because He *first* loved us." (1 John 4:19)

The whole procedure goes something like this: 1) *If we personally know that God loves us*; 2) we'll have the confidence and the trust to obey Him and lay our wills and our lives down before Him (i.e., become cleansed vessels); 3) and, because we are clean, we'll not only experience His Love personally, but also His Love through us to others; 4) and this, of course, gives us our meaning and purpose in life.

If however, 1) *we doubt God's personal Love*, then 2) we won't have the confidence or the trust to lay our wills and our lives down to Him (i.e., we'll be a clogged vessel), and 3) because His Spirit is quenched, it will limit our experiencing His Love, both personally and for others, which 4) of course, will affect our purpose and meaning in life.

There is a huge difference between God loving us and His being well pleased with us. He loved us even before we became believers—even when we were "dead in sin"—but He was not pleased with us. He becomes pleased with us when we trust, obey and follow Him. Many people often confuse these two and constantly try to earn His Love. This is not what He wants of us. We must serve Him totally out of a heart of love, *not in trying to earn His Love*. The latter is the philosophy of the world.

An Example: "I Want Out!"

Here's a perfect example: Sandy was a young Christian girl in her late twenties whom I met at a retreat in Northern California. She had had a very hard life and a very troubled background: drugs, alcohol, homosexuality and abuse.

When Sandy came up to the retreat in the mountains, she told God, "This is it. I can't go on anymore." She had become so despondent and so disillusioned with her life, her friends, her church and her family, that she decided if God didn't really love her, she wanted "out." She was already to the end of the enemy's **cycle of defeat**. She was giving up! Sandy begged God, "You have to show me that You really love me." She told Him that if she didn't see or hear anything that weekend, then she was going to take matters into her own hands.

Saturday afternoon, day two of the retreat, Sandy walked the grounds of the camp, contemplating how she might end her life.

That evening we had communion. By this time, Sandy was totally despondent. In desperation she told God she was going to refuse to take the communion cup until He somehow showed her that He loved her. Now, in general, it's not a good idea to give God an "ultimatum" like this. It's not Scriptural to do so. But God knew Sandy's heart and the desperate state that she was in.

After everyone had taken communion and left, Sandy moved up to the communion table. She quietly knelt down in front of the table, folded her arms on it and put her head down. She was determined to stay there until somehow she felt God's Love.

After she had knelt there for almost an hour, the doors in the back of the auditorium opened and someone came in. Sandy couldn't see who it was. The person quietly moved over to the fireplace, knelt down, and began to sing in the Spirit.[14] Later Sandy said that she "sang like an angel."

Sandy kept her head on the communion table for at least a half hour, while the singing continued. Finally, Sandy couldn't stand it any longer and came towards the fireplace to see who it was. The young girl seemed startled at first but then in an authoritative voice she told Sandy: "Sit down, God has sent me to you." Absolutely in shock, Sandy sat down, and they began to share.

The Lord had laid Sandy heavily upon this young girl's heart all weekend, but because she was a relatively new believer and Sandy had quite an intimidating countenance, she had kept her distance. In fact, she was a little frightened of Sandy. After the Saturday night session, she had gone to bed. She was almost asleep when she felt God directing her to get up and go minister to "someone in the main sanctuary who needed Him." Never dreaming it was Sandy, she rolled over and tried to ignore the Holy Spirit's prompting, but when no peace would come she got up, put on her robe and obeyed.

When she arrived in the auditorium she saw no one. But the Lord made her stay, wait and sing. When she saw Sandy coming around the corner, she was alarmed. But she immediately gave her fears over to the Lord, who calmly told her how to approach Sandy. The two young women shared all night long, crying, hugging and laughing together. God had, in His marvelous way shown Sandy the extent of His Love for her. And He used this precious new believer to do so.

The next morning, both girls got up in front of the entire women's group and shared what had happened. There wasn't a dry eye in the entire auditorium!

Can We Prove God Loves Us?

So knowing God loves us is critical. And since it's critical, is there some way we can prove it to those who don't understand His Love? Yes, I believe there is. While there are many ways, here are four of my favorites:

1) First, we can prove God loves us because *He says so in His Word.* Some Scriptures you might want to look up are: Jeremiah 31:3; Isaiah 43:4; 1 John 3:1; Psalm 18:4-6, 9, 16-19.

If you have difficulty really believing and intimately experiencing God's Love in your life, you might want to pick up the book *The Way of Agape* and see the supplement, *Knowing God Loves Me,* on page 351. Make up 3x5 cards with all the Scriptures noted there on how much God loves you. Keep these cards with you at all times—in your car, in your purse, on the mirror in the bathroom, etc. Then when doubt and unbelief overcome you, whip out those cards, confess your doubts and fears to the Lord, and then choose by faith—not feelings—to believe what God says. In His timing, God will align your feelings with those choices.

2) A second way we can prove that God loves us is that *He sent His Son to die for us that we might have life.* Jesus, God's Son, came in human flesh to take away our sins and to reconcile us to the Father. As 1 John 3:16 states, "By this we know Love, *because He laid down His life for us."* 1 John 4:10 also tells us that He was our *substitute offering.* He died in our place, so that we could be free from sin's penalty. The Bible tells us that there is no greater love than when a man lays down his life for his friends—exactly what Jesus did for us.

3)   Thirdly, we can prove God loves us because *He has sent His Holy Spirit to guide us, comfort us and equip us*. When we come into a new birth, ("born again"), God's Spirit unites with our human spirit and we are a new creation. (2 Corinthians 5:17) God's Spirit, given to indwell us, is like the down payment for or the guarantee, that His promises are true and trustworthy.

And, finally 4) we can prove God loves us because *He has given us His abundant life*: John 10:10 tells us that He came not only to give us life, but to give it to us abundantly! Abundant life means the supernatural Love, wisdom and power that we receive when we invite Christ into our hearts. John 3:16 tells us that we are simply partakers of His life. So, abundant life simply means experiencing Christ's life in place of our own. His Love becomes our love, His wisdom our wisdom and His power, our ability. Nothing in the entire world will convince us more that He does, indeed, love us.

If after reading the above reasons that prove God loves us, you *still* struggle with doubt, ask the Holy Spirit to bring a mature Christian into your life who can pray with you and encourage you through this critical juncture in your life.

An Example: Shar

Here's a personal example.

We spoke about Chip's death previously. Let me tell you about an experience I had just three weeks after he died. This incident proved to me beyond a shadow of a doubt that God loves me, that He has a perfect plan for my life, and that He yearns to give me His abundant life no matter what my circumstances.

Just 20 days after Chip passed on, there was a retreat scheduled in Chicago that I couldn't cancel. It would be too short a notice and too many people had already signed up to come. On the airplane, I told God I had absolutely *nothing* to give these women (I was totally empty), but I knew that He did and I was just willing to be an open vessel. I opened up the file for the seminar and immediately noticed a letter in that file from a woman named Shar, whom I had corresponded with a couple of times the previous year. The seminar "happened" to be at her own church.

Three years previously, Shar had lost her oldest son in a horrible automobile accident. He was only 20 at the time but loved the Lord with all his heart. Shar had been a Christian for years, had taught numerous Bible studies, and had exhorted many others to know Christ. But losing her son had absolutely crushed her. She could not understand how a loving God would allow such a tragedy to happen to a family who loved Him so much.

The more she questioned God, the more doubt and unbelief grew in her soul,—the enemy's **cycle of defeat**. As we said last chapter, doubt is the first step there and will affect everything we think, say and do. Eventually, Shar found herself at the lowest point in her walk with the Lord. **Defeat and despair**. When she prayed she couldn't hear His voice. When she read the Bible the enemy twisted its meaning to convey something totally opposite from what was intended. And when she went to Bible Studies, she didn't get anything out of them. So she just stopped praying, reading and going. **She gave up**! She felt God had covered Himself with a cloud in her deepest need and had abandoned her.

Shar became so depressed that she wanted to just die. She no longer cared about anything or anyone.

She dropped out of church, stopped seeing her friends and quit all social activities.

But the Lord, in His Love, had arranged this particular weekend not only to minister to me but also to show Shar just how much He loved her, and to what extremes He would go to communicate that Love to her.

I had last corresponded with Shar about a year *before* Chip died. In my letters I encouraged her as much as I possibly could and included passages like Romans 8:28 ("all things work together for good to those who love God"). However at that time, I really could not empathize with her because I had never walked in her shoes. *One year later, however, things radically changed...Chip died.*

And suddenly, on that plane, I knew "why" God was sending me there.

When I arrived in Chicago, I immediately called Shar and asked if she was going to the meeting that night. She said "no" and explained why. Then I told her about Chip. She had not heard. She began to cry. I, too, cried. But I told her that God had arranged this weekend and had sent me especially to her. He wanted the two of us that very night to go out under the stars and relinquish our sons to Him.

Shar came. And out of obedience, after the seminar was over, the two of us went outside, sat under the stars, and as best we could, gave our sons back to the Creator. The love that flowed between us and the Love we experienced from the Lord that night is something neither of us will ever forget. It was Christ's Love, His life, flowing between us, ministering to us, encouraging us and lifting us up. We felt Jesus, Himself, had come and touched us.

Shar is now back in church and fellowshipping, and, the last I heard, doing very well. God allowed still another very difficult night season in her life but, from what I hear, she has received it from God's hands and is glorifying Him through it. She didn't give up but is learning the fruit of longsuffering.

How Does God Communicate His Love?

Granted, you might say, so God loves us. But how, then, does He communicates that Love?

We can't box the Lord in. He will show us His Love in His own way and His own timing. But one of the first ways He does so is through His Word. This is where it all starts. This is how He talks to us, and this is how we hear His voice. Again, check out: Jeremiah 31:3; Isaiah 43:2-4; 1 John 3:1 and Psalm 18:4-6, 9, 16-19. Our responsibility is to choose, by faith, to believe what His Word says, knowing that in His perfect timing He will align our feelings to match that choice. But it all begins with reading His Word!

The next way the Lord communicates His Love is through Christian brothers and sisters, just as He did with Shar and me. We are a family. We are extensions of His Love to each other. He is constantly giving us opportunities to allow Him to love others through us. Thus, it's important that when you are asked to pray for a person, be faithful to do so. We must also be willing to do anything else the Lord might lay on our hearts—call, write a note, visit, take a gift or make some other personal sacrifice. Each time we let God use us in a personal way, it's a touch from Him, saying to that person, "I love you."

A third way that God communicates His Love to us is *through situations and circumstances*. There is nothing quite so wonderful and comforting as knowing that God has personally orchestrated our circumstances.   However we must be very careful here, because often in difficult situations there are very few "outward" signs of a loving Father. But, if we are really looking, *we should be able to see His handprint of Love getting us through those difficulties*.

An Example: Gifts From the Heart

Here's another personal example:

I was one of those very fortunate people to have had an "ideal" mom. We were best friends for over 60 years, with never a harsh word between us.

November 2000, we found out Mom, who was 86, had pancreatic cancer with only a few weeks to live. I immediately flew to Northern California to be with her. By December she was so sick that we had to place her in Hospice, a beautiful facility for the terminally ill. I stayed at my brother's weekend house, which was only three minutes away, so that I could visit her two and three times a day.

My brother, when he could, would come down on weekends; but his own family lived in San Francisco and, because it was the holidays, he could not come as often as he wanted.

Even though Mom was still in the hospital, the people who owned Mom's apartment knew that she would not be returning, so they asked if we would move her things, since they had a chance to lease it to someone else. My brother and sister-in-law came down and helped, but they had to leave early to get back to their family for Christmas. So *the night before Christmas*, I found myself alone in Mom's empty apartment, packing up a few treasures that she had already designated for my brother and me. (She had absolutely beautiful things—antique treasures from my grandparents and great grandparents and from her travels all over the world—all labeled with dates, historical descriptions and whom they were to go to.)

As I was packing these beautiful treasures, the thought struck me that throughout my whole life Mom and Dad had always made our Christmases special. They loved the holidays and they always made such a big deal about them. Even after I married, they would come to our home with their arms loaded with gifts. They continued to do this till the year my Dad died.

This particular year, however, because Mom had been so sick and because it had been such a difficult time for my own family financially, we (the Missler's) had decided not to exchange at all. The thought struck me: Here it was the night before Christmas and my precious Mom was *again* making our Christmas special. She was still alive, so there was no sting of death; and yet, again, she was giving us all gifts of love from her heart.

God had arranged it that way. Now, it didn't have to be Christmas Eve; it could have been July or August or March. There was only a *1-in-365* chance that it would be Christmas. To me, it was God's perfect orchestration,—His handprint of Love helping me to get through a most difficult circumstance.

Mom went home to be with the Lord January 4th. The next day "happened" to be my birthday and, coincidently, the same day we were to read her will and open her safe deposit box. Now, neither my brother nor I knew what was inside that box. But when we opened it, we found the most incredible love letters to both of us, telling us *how much she loved us and how we would always be in her heart*. And, in my love letter, was a birthday gift that I will never forget. She told me that she wanted me to have her beautiful gold ring with a diamond cross on it that my father had made especially for her on their 50th wedding anniversary.

It's something I will always cherish and will always wear to remind me of my Proverbs 31 mom. Again, only God could have orchestrated this to happen *on my birthday* (again a *1-in-365* chance to be so). God's handprint of Love!

Truly God is involved in every single aspect of our lives if we are looking; and there is no sorrow so great that He cannot somehow recycle it to bring forth a blessing.

No Fear in God's Love

God's Love is our foundation, our building pad and the rock upon which we build our whole spiritual house. Without this foundation our lives would crumble. Hope in His Love is what gives us faith to see beyond the near term, beyond the current situation, beyond the problems and look to Christ for our final victory. If we really knew how much God loves us, there would *never* be any reason to fear what He might allow into our lives.

We each need to get to the point in our walks with the Lord where we can say and *mean*, "Because *I know You love me*, even if You slay me, I will trust You." (Job 13:15) In other words, even though everything in my life is turned upside down, I will still trust You because I know You love me!

How Much Do You Trust God?

If you are in the middle of a very difficult situation, and doubt and unbelief have already crept into your thinking, then don't wait another moment. Turn to the Lord right now. Make the appropriate "faith choices" to give all the confusion, dismay and disappointment over to Him; and say, as did the father of the ill child in Mark 9:24, "Lord, I believe, *help my unbelief.*"

Remember the enemy is waiting to take you down his **cycle of defeat**. *Doubt* leads to *discouragement*, which breeds *confusion*, which produces *depression, loss of vision, disorientation* and, eventually, *complete despair* and *defeat*. In short, wanting totally to give up! God, on the other hand, wants you to choose His **cycle of trust**. *Knowing His Love* produces *your obedience*, which brings about *His presence* and *the ability to persevere through any trial*. In other words, the God-given ability to never give up!

So, the first step in God's **cycle of trust** is knowing how much He loves us. Ask Him to prove it to you through His Word, through others and by seeing His handprint of Love even in your difficult circumstances. If you are looking, I promise you will see Him!

The God of the Bible is a loving and compassionate Father, who will use all the events in our lives to rid us of sin and self, so that He might replace us with Himself. He continually is stretching and shaping our faith so that we will be able to endure any circumstance, and say with absolute conviction, "Though [You] slay me, yet will I *trust* [You]." (Job 13:15)

Isaiah 43:2-4 tells us that when we pass through the waters (trouble), He will be with us; and through the rivers, they shall not overflow us: when we walk through the fire, we will not be burned: neither shall the flame kindle upon us. For, He tells us, 'You are precious in My sight and *I love you.*'

Therefore, we are not to fear, because <u>He</u> is with us!

"Though He were a Son, yet learned He obedience by the things which He suffered." (Hebrews 5:8)

Chapter 3
In Obedience, Learning to Love God

Learning Obedience Through Longsuffering

In the eye of the storm, we constantly have two major choices facing us: God's **cycle of trust** (unconditionally trusting Him, which leads to sight and the ability to endure), or the enemy's **cycle of defeat** (emotionally doubting the Lord, which leads to confusion and devastation and the feeling of giving up). These two choices will always be ours, and ours alone, to make.

The first two steps in God's **cycle of trust** are knowing His will and knowing He loves us. These two principles go hand in hand, and we'll learn that we cannot proceed further unless we are "living them," experiencing them and embracing them, not just in our heads, but in our everyday life actions. These two steps are the foundation blocks or the corner stones of our Christian walk. Without them, we will not be able to go on to obeying, loving and seeing Him who is invisible! As we said before, all these principles intertwine and depend upon each other. Knowing God's will and knowing that He loves us allows us to go on to the next step, which is obeying Him.

We show our trust in the Lord by our obedience—i.e., by doing in action what He has asked.

I remember, as a young Christian, hearing about all the Old Testament saints and how it was only *after* they took that step of obedience, that He manifested Himself to them. And, because they obeyed Him, they were able to go on and do incredible things *for* Him. Did they always "feel like" doing what He asked of them? I certainly don't think so. I don't think Abraham "felt like" sacrificing his only son. (Genesis 22) I don't think Moses "felt like" leaving his family and fleeing into the wilderness. And, I don't think Joseph "felt like" serving in Potiphar's house or being in prison for years. No, all of these men did so purely out of *obedience*! And, because they obeyed, God manifested Himself to them.

So, obedience always comes *before* sight. Only *after* I take that step of obedience, does God reveal Himself to me.

So, the response that God desires when a trial or tragedy hits, is for us to trust Him enough to obey Him. No matter what we see happening or how we feel, we must *unconditionally trust His Love and take that obedient step,* knowing that somehow and someway He will use our situation for our good and His glory.

To obey God simply means continually to set aside and relinquish what we think, what we want and what pleases us; and, by faith choose to do whatever He has asked. I've learned the hard way that obedience is the *only* answer. I've learned to obey God even when it's the last thing in the world that I want to do. I have tried all the other ways and *obedience* truly is the only way that works.

I've learned that I must obey, because only then will God be free to work out the circumstances in my life according to His will. Until I choose to obey, those circumstances are still *my* responsibility. But once I choose to relinquish myself over to Him, those circumstances then become His responsibility.

An Example: Raw Eggs

Here's a silly, but graphic personal example:

Many years ago, Chuck and I had an evening planned at the Music Center in Los Angeles with some very important business friends who were non-believers. Because we lived in Orange County and it was at least an hour's drive to Los Angeles, we had to pick up these friends by five o'clock in order to make dinner on time.

As it happened, that day was my carpool day for Michelle. I figured if I got all the girls home by 3:30 p.m., I'd still have plenty of time to get dressed and pick up our friends by five.

That afternoon, however, one of the little girls in the carpool smashed her finger in the car door as she was getting in. We had to rush her back into school, soak her finger, call her mother and do some T.L.C. (tender loving care). I lost half an hour there.

When Michelle and I finally got home, I noticed a horrible smell coming from the back of the car. It turned out to be a whole carton of spilled and spoiled milk that one of the little girls had forgotten. Since this was the car I was using that evening, I needed to do an extra special job of cleaning up the mess so it wouldn't stink. I lost another 15 minutes here. (I think the Lysol smell was probably worse than that of the spoiled milk!)

When I finished cleaning the car, I rushed into the house to make a soufflé. I was hosting a luncheon the next day for twelve women, and I needed to make some last-minute preparations. (The soufflé needed to be made a day in advance in order to refrigerate overnight.)

I have one special pan that I use for a soufflé; none of my other pans work. For some reason, that day I couldn't find it. After spending ten anxious minutes opening and shutting all the cupboards in my kitchen, trying to find my pan, I remembered we had lent our house to some people over Christmas. I thought perhaps by mistake they had taken it home. I called, and after several minutes of chit chat, the wife verified that, yes, she had my pan. She said she could return it the next day. "No, thank you," I said, "that's too late; I need it now. Thank you anyway."

By now it was 4:15 p.m.! I wasn't dressed, the soufflé wasn't made, the kids weren't fed, and I was beginning to get a little panicked. I took out another pan, threw in all the ingredients and tried to stir. But the bowl was too small and I couldn't mix it properly. In desperation, I threw the whole mixture (a quart of milk, a dozen eggs, mustard, Worcestershire sauce, etc.) into my new Cuisinart, not realizing that liquids can't go above the two-inch tube in the center or they will overflow. And, that's exactly what happened!

Twelve raw eggs and one quart of milk began to ooze out all over the counter, down the sides of the cabinets, into the drawers, down my legs, into my shoes, and onto the floor. It was now 4:30 p.m. By this time I was totally out of control! I began to scream, kick, and yell. (Have you ever been there? Can you identify?)

God gently tapped me on the shoulder and asked, "Nancy, will you choose right now to obey Me? Do you love Me that much?" God wanted me to choose, at that very moment, to relinquish my anger, my frustration, and my anxiety to Him, and not allow those wild emotions to direct my actions anymore.

Do you know how hard it is, in the middle of a "fit," to stop, turn around, and choose to act in a calm manner? It's impossible; it's totally supernatural!

But, as I have said, I have learned over all these years that I have been a Christian, that no other way works. I literally have tried *every* other way possible and none works. So out loud, almost crying, right there in the middle of the egg yolks, I made that commitment to God that I would obey Him. Now I certainly didn't feel like it; it was totally a faith choice, a non-feeling choice. I consciously relinquished my anger, my frustrations, and all of my distraught feelings. I confessed that they were obviously not of faith and were therefore sin. And I asked Him to purge them from me.

In other words, I barred myself from following my unruly feelings by determining not to give in to them; instead, giving them to God and doing what He was asking me to do. Then I asked God to help me get ready on time, to pick up our friends by five, and even to be a genuine representation of Him that evening.

God is so faithful. I ran upstairs and was able to find a perfect outfit to wear. I jumped in the shower and did what I could with my disheveled hair. I was only 15 minutes late picking those people up that night, and yet we were right on time for the dinner and the show in Los Angeles!

The best part of the whole evening was experiencing God's Love, not only for me personally, but flowing through me that night to our friends. Can you imagine what kind of a Godly representative I would have been had I not made that choice to obey God?

I think I fed the ladies sandwiches the next day.

Three Steps of Obedience

Now, since the word 'obedience' is such a very broad term, let's narrow it down just a bit. There are three essential parts to obeying God within His **cycle of trust**. They are: 1) out of obedience, we must learn to "love" (*agapao*) God; 2) out of obedience, we must learn how to moment-by-moment renew our minds; and 3) out of obedience, we must learn how to have unshakeable faith in all circumstances.

Again, at first glance, you might think, "Oh, those are easy! I'm already doing them! What's so new?" I assure you, however, that not one of these three principles is easy nor what you might imagine! Most of us haven't the faintest idea of what the Bible really means when it says we are "to love God." Most of us think that simply means affection love. But nothing could be further from the truth. And renewing our minds is *far more* than what one might first expect. Did you know the battle for our lives is really waged in our minds? Or that *if we don't learn how to renew our minds daily, the enemy will end up in control?* And finally, naked faith is not only trusting what God does *through* us, it's also trusting what He does *towards* us.

So let's take a look at each of these three principles of obedience and see how we can learn to respond as God would have us do.

Learn to Love God

One of the first ways we must learn to obey God in our trials is to learn to love Him more and not pull away from Him. Now, again, that sounds so easy and so simple and, as I said, most of us would probably say, "But, I already love Him! What's to learn?" Well, loving God the way Scripture tells us is <u>not</u> easy, nor is it simple and most of us are <u>not</u> doing it!

The Greek word for 'love,' used in both of the great commandments, is the verb *agapao*. (Matthew 22:37-39) *Agapao* means to totally give ourselves over to something; to be totally consumed with it; or to be totally committed to it. In other words, what we *agapao* is what we put first in our lives. All our intentions and abilities are focused and consumed with this one thing. To *agapao* something means to bind ourselves to it so that we become almost "one." Ultimately, what we *agapao* is that to which we willingly submit our wills and lives.

Now, this commitment love—totally giving ourselves over to something—can either be to God, to man or to things of the world. We, of course, obviously think we are loving God first, but if I asked you, "How often do you seek to put <u>His</u> will and <u>His</u> desires above your own? How often are you consumed with what <u>He</u> desires for your life and not what you want out of life? *Can you honestly say that you desire His will above your own happiness?* How about in a trial?

If your answer is yes to the above questions, then, perhaps you *are* loving Him the way He desires. But, if your answer is "no," then you might want to read on...

An Example: A Total Miracle

Let me give you a perfect example of a Christian woman who, in the worst of times, chose to love God obediently and put His will and desires above her own.

Many years ago, Heidi found herself in a very hurtful marriage. However, she was absolutely convinced that God wanted her to stay in it, regardless of how her husband treated her. There was no physical abuse or adultery; he simply no longer loved her and wanted her out of his life. He had tired of her and was doing everything he could to make her life miserable, so that *she* would be the one to file for divorce.

Now, certainly Heidi would have been much happier out of the marriage and away from the constant harassments. Yet, she knew that God had not given her permission to leave. And *she was more concerned about doing God's perfect will than she was about her own momentary happiness.*

Sometime later, I happened to see Heidi at a party, and she had incredible news. God had totally changed her husband's heart. He had repented, come under a pastor's care and counsel, and was now doing everything he could to make things up to her. In time, God restored their marriage completely. It was a total miracle, but I believe much of it occurred because Heidi was more concerned about being obedient and loving God, than she was her own momentary happiness.

I'm sure some of you are wondering when you read the above story, if you ever will have a "Heidi Miracle." Well, it's totally up to you and the Lord. But even if your spouse never changes, never softens and never turns around, as long as you keep in the Lord's 'cycle of trust,' your life can still flow with "rivers of living water." (John 7:38) I'm convinced God can turn our sorrows into blessings.

This unconditional surrender is what it means to love (*agapao*) God! But, this attitude is very difficult to find in the Christian Body today. Selfishness and self-centeredness seems to be the present agenda. Many Christians are not willing to set aside what they want and what they feel in order to do what God has asked. In general, the majority of Christians are seeking their own happiness and their own fulfilment. Is this your goal? Or is it to set yourself aside and love God? Everything in your life depends upon this one decision, this one choice. Will you love Him first, or are you going to give yourself over to what you want, feel and think?

Loving God First

When a trial or tragedy hits, the natural and emotional thing for us to do is to let go, give in and give up, simply because we're disappointed, confused and hurt at what the Lord has allowed. This, of course, is the opposite of what we *should* do and precisely what the enemy wants us to do. When we pull away and isolate ourselves, the enemy wins! *Just as the wolf lures its prey out of the pack, so Satan wants to kill, steal and destroy us by isolation and vulnerability.* Remember his **cycle of defeat**. Trials are the most important time for us to pull in even closer to the Lord, trust Him implicitly and love (*agapao*) Him even more.

We must learn to love God without the need to see or understand exactly what He is doing. Read that again. The only thing we need to understand in our trial is not what God is doing, but what He expects from us. If we know and are living His **cycle of trust**, we'll not only make it through, we'll free Him to work miracles.

Romans 8:28 takes on a whole new light here. "And we know that all things work together for good to them that love God." It follows that, "all things work together for good" to those who totally give themselves over to Him (*agapao*), but not to those who only have affection (*storge*) for Him.

So, to *agapao* God is <u>not</u> an emotional feeling. Many of us thought this is what loving God meant. Yet, this is not to say that when we are truly loving Him—totally giving ourselves over to Him by laying our wills and our lives down to Him—we won't be emotionally involved. We will! But we *can't* run our relationship with Him, or with others, on feelings. If we do, our lives will be on a continual roller coaster, totally dependent upon emotions, circumstances and how we're treated. We've all been there and it doesn't work! No, to love God the way He desires means a moment-by-moment surrender of our total self (all of our thoughts, emotions, and desires *that are contrary to His*). When we do this, His life can come forth from our hearts and His Love can be extended to others *through* us.

2 Corinthians 4:10-11 expresses it well, "For we who live are always delivered unto death for Jesus' sake, that the life also of Jesus might be made manifest in our mortal flesh."

To Love God Is To Lose Self

To totally give ourselves over to Him simply means to choose to give to God anything in our lives that is not of faith. (2 Corinthians 10:3-6) Now, when I say totally giving ourselves over to Him or surrendering self, I don't mean losing who we really are and becoming some sort of a mindless robot. I simply mean setting aside all our own thoughts, emotions, and desires *that are contrary to God's*, and becoming a cleansed and open vessel so that His life can flow. Then, He can use us as vessels to love others. If, however, we are holding on to bitterness, resentment, anger (even if "justified" by worldly standards), His Spirit will be quenched in us and He won't be able to use us.

Remember John 12:24: "...Except a corn of wheat fall into the ground and die, it abideth alone: but if it die, it bringeth forth much fruit." The glorious fruit of God's Love!

The problem is that we often don't see ourselves as Jesus does. We think we're in great shape and there's no stumbling block in us. Consequently, in order to reveal our true heart condition, the Lord must allow circumstances into our lives that force us to see our wrong priorities and our wrong dependencies. In other words, *He pushes us into a corner* where we come face to face with what we truly are. We must "see" our self-life for ourselves, in order to make the necessary choices to give it over to Him.

The Gospel is not *health and wealth* in this life, but a call to follow in Jesus Christ's footsteps. He has left us an incredible example. He was rejected by those He came to save, and then crucified that we might be saved, loved and have life! This is the example He left for us and the pattern He wants us to follow. *To love Him means to lose ourselves!* As someone told me yesterday, we should ask God everyday, "Whom do You want me to give my life away to today?"

An Example: "There was not a 'Me' there."

Here's a great example of this:

I have a dear Christian friend named Sue. After a painful divorce, Sue decided to move to the East Coast. Her estranged husband Jim, who was Jewish, continued to live in Southern California with his new girlfriend, Joy.

A year or so after the divorce, Sue had to come back to California on a business trip. She could hardly wait to see all of her old friends again. She found out that there was a party being planned and she was so looking forward to seeing "the old gang," most of whom were Jewish.

After she arrived in California, someone called Sue and told her that her ex-husband Jim and his girlfriend were also going to be at the party. Feeling extremely angry and upset, Sue thought to herself, "How dare they invite Jim and his girlfriend as well as me. There is just no way in the world I am going to that party now."

For one entire week Sue argued with God, knowing that God would have her give Him her hurts, resentments, and bitternesses, and then trust Him. Sue knew in her heart that God wanted to use her at that party. She knew He wanted to pour out His Love on these precious Jewish people who didn't *know* Him. However, sometimes we just cannot make the choice to give ourselves over to God right away. Sometimes it just feels good to "feel sorry" for ourselves for awhile and wade in the muck and mire of self-pity. Do you know what I mean? Have you ever been there?

God is so wonderful, though. He loves us even through our temper tantrums and even when we are being brats. He patiently waits by us, never leaving us or forsaking us, until we just can't stand the "pig sty" any longer and we give in and choose to do it His way.

That's just what happened with Sue. After an entire week of wrestling with God, He convinced her that it *was* His will that she attend the party and carry His Love.

After finally reconciling herself to the Lord's desires, Sue told God, "Okay, I'm willing to go to that party; I'm willing to give you my hurts and my past memories and become an open vessel; but it's totally impossible for me to extend love to those at the party. You're going to have to do that for me."

That's all God wanted. When Sue arrived at the party house, the first person she met at the door was Jim's girlfriend, Joy. Sue said later, "It was absolutely wild! My body stayed outside the door when it opened, but something deep within me stepped inside, reached out to Joy and in total genuineness said, "I am so glad to meet you. I really have heard so many nice things about you" (which was true).

Joy and Sue sat on the couch talking comfortably for about an hour and a half. Jim must have sensed Sue's openness and genuine concern, because he, later asked Sue if they could go into another room and talk privately. Sensing her genuine compassion, Jim felt free to share from his heart many intimate things about their marriage.

When Sue was relating this story to me over the phone, I stopped her and asked, "But, Sue, how did you feel when Jim began to share all those painful things?" Her immediate response was: "Nancy, it was incredible, *there was not a 'me' there.*" Sue was so completely one with God at that moment that it was God's character and His life that flowed through her, rather than her own. 1 John 4:17 declares that, "*as He is, so are we [to be] in this world.*"

Sometimes it may only be for a moment that we stay open and cleansed so God's Love can flow through us. That's okay, because tomorrow it may be for five minutes and the next day perhaps ten.

So remember this story: *to love God means to lose self.*

This kind of love is a different kind of love than what you thought, isn't it?

Isn't There Any Other Way?

Many years ago, a couple of young moms came running up to me after a seminar and said, "Oh Nan, we're scared! Is it only through trials and tribulations that we learn to walk as Jesus walked? Isn't there any other way that we can learn this?" These two young women were very content with their lives as they were. They had prospering husbands, beautiful homes and young families. They were frightened as to what God might do.

"First of all," I told them, "Remember God loves you. And, remember, He loves your husbands and your children far more than you could ever understand and, thus, He won't allow anything in your lives that's not *Father filtered*." Then I quickly added, "I do believe that we <u>can</u> learn to walk as Jesus walked without any trials in our lives *if we only would be willing to totally give ourselves over to Him in <u>every</u> situation. If we did this, there would be no need for trials in our lives.*"

They understood completely and went away at peace.

The real truth, however, is that *very few* of us will ever voluntarily make this kind of total commitment. Our human nature is to *preserve ourselves* and to *hold on to ourselves* at all costs. In fact, our human nature constantly screams to get its own way. Selfishness and self-centeredness rule the day! And unless we are *cornered* by God through difficult circumstances, we probably would just continue going our own way forever. *Brokenness is God's way of turning us around and making us see for ourselves the need for transformation.*

Love As Jesus Loved

Throughout the New Testament, Jesus commands us not only to love Him, but also to unconditionally love others. These are the two great commandments in which the whole Bible is summed up. Thus, a part of our learning obedience is to learn to totally give ourselves over to others. We'll talk more about this later, but learning to unconditionally love others will increase our capability to patiently endure our trials.

In John 13:34 Jesus says, "A new commandment I give unto you, that ye love one another; *as I have loved you*, that ye also love one another."

How did Jesus love us? He laid down His life for us! He loved us so much that He died for us. This is the example that God has set down for us and that He desires we follow. It was only because of God's voluntary death that His *Agape* Love could be given to us. And it's only when we choose to die to our self life that God's unconditional Love can be manifested through us to others.

This is the substance of the Second Commandment. If we love God first, above all else, He will then enable us to love others *before or instead of,* ourselves. Because we are open vessels, He will pour His Love *through us* and give us the ability to put others' needs before our own.

An Example: "Me, Wash His Feet?"

Here's a beautiful example.

At the time of the following incident, Melissa and her husband, Walt, had four small children under the age of seven.

Melissa had become extremely exhausted caring for all the needs of her small children, and so had begun to pray that Walt would be more sensitive to her needs, helping out more with the kids when he got home in the afternoon. He was a medical technician who went to work around 6 a.m. and came home between 2 p.m. and 3 p.m. Melissa prayed this prayer for some time, without any visible results.

One evening Walt came home early only to find the house a total mess. He had to step over dirty laundry, broken toys, and what was left of lunch, in order to find his way upstairs to Melissa and the kids. She had all four children in the bathtub, washing their hair. Walt stuck his head in the door and asked, "What on earth is going on? Why is the house such a mess?"

Now, since Melissa had been entertaining such thoughts as "Why can't Walt help me more? and I just can't take this any longer!", she immediately reacted out of those frustrations and shouted, "Well, if you would only help me more with these kids, I'd have more time to clean *your* house!" Obviously, it was not a response out of God's Love but one triggered by her own built-up resentment.

Poor Walt was terribly hurt. He immediately became defensive and said something else about her messy house. She retaliated with another jab. More words were exchanged, and then Walt slammed the bathroom door and started downstairs, mumbling something like "Boy, it's great to be home."

Melissa finished putting the kids to bed, shushing their inquisitive little questions of "Is Daddy mad at us?" and "Why did Daddy slam the door, Mommie?"

After tucking the kids in bed, Melissa went downstairs. Not wanting to be in the same room with

Walt (ever felt that way?), she went to the opposite end
of the house, got out her Bible and began to pour out
her true feelings to God. She started to cry and told
God how tired, how lonely, and how unhappy she was,
feeling as if Walt didn't even care about her anymore.
He seemed, at times, so distant and insensitive.

After weeping quietly for a long time she told God,
*"But, I do really love You and I want to obey You and
do what is right.* What would you have me to do?"
God's still, small voice directed her to Matthew 16:24:
"If any man will come after Me, let him deny himself,
pick up his cross, and follow Me." Melissa sat there
for a long time contemplating how on earth this verse
applied to her situation. Again God's still, small voice
said, *"If you will love me first, I'll enable you to love
your husband."*

Melissa immediately replied, "But Lord, I do love
You. How else am I supposed to show You? What else
am I supposed to do?" With that, God impressed upon
her mind, "If you really love Me, then get a basin of
water and go and wash your husband's feet."

Well, you can imagine her reaction! If it were you,
what would be your reaction? Her's was the same.
"Are you kidding? After what he's said and done to
me, *he* should be the one to wash my feet!"

God was silent. Finally Melissa began to
understand, for the first time, what it really meant to
love God: to deny yourself, pick up your cross and
follow Him. God was asking her not only to deny
what she wanted, but He was also asking her to get
up and do something she absolutely didn't want to do,
which was to wash Walt's feet. God was asking her to
do what Jesus would do in that situation.

Melissa had been studying about *Agape* Love and she knew if she didn't obey God and do what He was asking her, she would quench His Spirit (His Love) in her heart. She couldn't stand that. So she made the difficult faith choice, got up, got a bowl of water and a towel from the kitchen and went into her husband's study. Walt was lying on the couch, reading. She knelt down quietly beside him and began to untie his shoes, crying softly as she did. At first, she said, she didn't feel a thing, for it was totally a faith choice with no feelings. But, by the time she began to take off his shoes and socks, it had become pure genuine love. God had aligned her feelings to match her faith choices.

Walt was flabbergasted when he saw Melissa walk into the room with that bowl of water. *He was sure it was going to be thrown over his head!* But when he saw her tears and felt her genuine love, he reached down and drew her up to himself. And they were reconciled—both emotionally and spiritually.

Holding and embracing one another and truly realizing how much they really loved each other, Melissa was able to share with Walt her deepest needs. Because she was at this point a cleansed vessel, Walt heard her from his heart and not his defenses. The next several months became a special time in their marriage where they both became more sensitive to each other's needs with Walt helping her more with the kids, and Melissa trying to insure a loving atmosphere when he came home at night.

A dear, dear friend of mine just wrote me a letter sharing a similar story: "I have learned over the last several months as the trials have increased in our family, to personally apply "loving as Jesus loved." When I choose to put myself and my selfish desires aside, things at home change dramatically. I now say to myself when I come home and see everything a mess, 'my wife must have had a rough day, I need to bless her.' Thus, rather than walking in and commenting on what is <u>not</u> done (housework, cleaning, meals, children, etc.), I kiss my wife and children and tell them how special they are to me. My wife's reply immediately changes from, 'if you only had...then, I would have...' to 'I'm sorry the house is such a mess.' It's a phenomenal change of heart. Remember, it's very difficult for a strong-willed man, like myself, to line up with what God wants. (*I know what He wants*, I just don't want to do it.) However, as I yield myself totally to Him, all of us are blessed. And, even our sex life is impacted!!!"

Denying Ourselves

The Scripture that God gave Melissa that afternoon was Matthew 16:24: "If any man will come after Me, let him *deny himself*, pick up his cross and follow Me."

Now, *"to deny ourselves"* in God's economy doesn't mean to deny "outward" things (i.e., houses, cars, fashionable clothing, etc.). This sort of denial is actually a lot easier! Rather, to deny ourselves means to relinquish "inward" things (i.e., our own "justified" thoughts, *our expectations*, our emotions and our desires for success that are usually contrary to God's). And, this step, at least for me, is much harder.

Also, to deny does not mean to push down and bury our "real" feelings, nor negate the existence of our true emotions and pretend that they don't exist. No, to deny ourselves means to bar ourselves from following these negative thoughts and feelings and to prevent ourselves from being influenced by them.

We're all human and we all will have negative thinking until we see Jesus. To deny ourselves simply means to look at these things, to call them for what they are and then give them to the Lord. It means to "bar ourselves" from following what these negative things are telling us and, instead, do what God has asked. Remember, the definition of the word *suffering*—to bar ourselves from following what we think, feel and desire, and instead, doing what God wants. Hebrews 5:8 tells us that we learn obedience through the things we suffer. Denying ourselves validates this same principle. When we deny ourselves, we often do suffer because our "flesh" is dying.

Again, this is one of God's purposes for allowing trials in our lives—to break us of *our* own self-centeredness and to fill us with *His* other-centeredness.

An Example: Sarah and Pastor Paul

Here's a striking example of this:

When I think about trusting, obeying and loving God (and becoming totally other-centered), I can't help but think of Sarah, a dear friend of mine. Sarah is a pastor's wife who has been married for many, many years, has helped her husband pastor several churches, has four grown children and ten grandchildren.

About a year ago Paul, her husband, became very discouraged and distant. Sarah recognized it, but nothing she said seemed to help. Then, one day, Paul just left.

Precious Sarah, rather than get angry, scream and yell at Paul, she obediently went to the Lord and asked Him what she was to do. What did He want her to do?

What was <u>His</u> will in all of this? She was confident that God loved her and that He was completely aware of her situation. The Lord was very clear in His answer. He told her to surrender all, keep praying and "be obedient in <u>all</u> things." He told her to *never give up* hoping and trusting in Him.

Every time she would speak to her husband, she would say, "I know God is in our marriage. I still love you and I see no Scriptural basis for what you are doing." This response totally convicted her husband, because he knew in his spirit she was right! Her Godly responses would not allow him to "justify" what he was doing. Instead, her reaction heaped "coals of fire" on his head, just as Romans 12:20 tells us.

Even though she felt completely rejected, Sarah chose over and over again, to stay in God's **cycle of trust**—allowing **God's Love** to produce an **obedience in her** which resulted in **God's presence** and the ability **to persevere**. A Scripture that fits Sarah perfectly is Psalm 44:17-18 (paraphrased): All this is come upon me; yet I have <u>not</u> forgotten Thee, neither have I dealt falsely in Thy covenant. My heart is <u>not</u> turned back, neither have my steps declined from Thy way."

Sarah **never let go**, **never gave in** and **never gave up**! She kept walking in the midst of the fire. Months went by. From the world's point of view, it was completely over. But precious Sarah continued to pray, continued to stand strong and continued to be obedient. She chose daily, by faith, to give God all her hurts, anger and resentments, so she could unconditionally forgive and love (with God's Love) her wayward husband. Talk about a "living example" of longsuffering, Sarah has shown us how it is to be done!

God was faithful. Eventually Pastor Paul was home. He was literally prayed home by his 1 Corinthians 13 wife who "never gave up" hope. The family is now in the process of a full restoration and under pastoral care.

The lesson for us is that if Sarah could remain steadfast and full of the Lord's Spirit in her situation, then any of us can. Obedience is the only answer. We must obey God by *first* learning to love Him—totally giving ourselves over to Him in all things. Then, He will give us the love we need to become totally other-centered. "Nothing is impossible with God"— especially if we are *sold out* to Him and committed to reflecting Him, as was Sarah.

Sarah's suggestion for all of us is to "listen for the Lord's will in everything; and don't lean on your own understanding."

He Is Our Life

It's imperative we learn to love the Lord, without the need to see or understand exactly what He is doing. The only thing we need to understand in our trials is not what He is doing, but *what He expects from us*. This, then, frees Him to work miracles in our lives, even in our darkest times.

Loving God is *not* an emotional feeling, nor is it an emotional high; rather it's a complete surrender of ourselves. Loving God is the oneness, the union and the marriage relationship that He desires with every one of us. One heart, one will and one life. He wants each of us to be so "at one" with Him that what others see and hear through us are His Love, His wisdom and His power. His image only, not our own.

God's will—transformation into His image—is accomplished by *first* knowing He loves us, then by our obediently loving Him in return.

The inward life of the spirit can only be gained by a passionate and consuming love for God. How much do you love Him? Enough to patiently endure what He has allowed in your life? This is a question each of us must answer for ourselves. The walk of faith necessary for experiencing His presence is <u>not</u> easy and it's not quick. It's not only going through the narrow gate, but it's patiently enduring the hard path. In the words of Jesus, "Narrow is the gate and hard is the way, which leadeth unto life, and few there be that find it." (Matthew 7:14)

How about you? Have you found it?

(If you have enjoyed this chapter and want to learn more about loving God, I would recommend our book *The Way of Agape*. It's a complete textbook on the how to love God and others.)

"*...put off* concerning your former conduct, the old man, which grows corrupt according to the deceitful lusts, and *be renewed in the spirit of your mind*; and *put on* the new man, which after God is created in righteousness and true holiness."
(Ephesians 4:22-24)

Chapter 4
In Obedience, Learning to Renew Your Mind

Review

So far in our exploration of longsuffering and God's **cycle of trust** to achieve it, we have talked about the importance of knowing God's will, His Love and the critical necessity of being obedient. We shared that there are *several* steps of obedience that we must take everyday and sometimes many times a day: choosing to love Him; choosing to renew our minds; and choosing to have unshakeable faith. In the last chapter we covered what it means to love Him, totally giving ourselves over to Him. Now let's talk about what it means to moment-by-moment renew our minds.

More than any other time in our lives, during a personal trial is the time that we need to know how to "put off our old thinking" and "put on the new." Romans 12:1-2 emphasizes the importance of doing this. It tells us that the only thing that will bring about a transformed life, which is Jesus' Life through us, is a renewed mind. *Instruction will <u>not</u> bring about transformation; knowledge does <u>not</u> bring it about; nor, does wisdom. Only a renewed mind transforms us into Christ's image.*

What Is A Renewed Mind?

Now what exactly is a renewed mind? How do we get one? And what are the practical steps to doing so?

Renewing our minds simply means "putting off" the garbage in our thinking and "putting on" the Mind of Christ. It's <u>not</u> just changing our thoughts but actually *putting off* the old negative ones while *putting on* the new, Godly ones. In a moment of trial we cannot simply say to the Lord, "Please, give me Your thoughts" and expect somehow to read His mind. It doesn't work that way. We must *first* choose to "put off" all our own self-centered thinking by *confessing it, repenting of it* and *giving it to Him.* Then, and only then, can we put on the mind of Christ.

Ephesians 4:22-24 tells us that we are to: *"put off* concerning the former conversation [our behavior] the old man [the old self], which is corrupt according to the deceitful lusts, And *be renewed in the spirit of your mind*; And *put on* the new man [the new self], which after God is created in righteousness and true holiness."

A renewed mind is characterized by two things: one, it has *put off* any sin—any thought, any emotion or any desire that is not of faith—and, two, it has *put on* the Mind of Christ—His wisdom, His understanding, His knowledge etc. See Isaiah 11:2 for a full description of the attributes or characteristics of the Mind of Christ.

A renewed mind is the means by which God's life (His *Agape* Love, His wisdom and power), already resident in our hearts (if we are born again), is manifested out in our day-to-day living. In other words, a renewed mind is the *vehicle* by which God's Love in our hearts becomes our love in our souls, His thoughts become our thoughts and His wisdom, our wisdom.

An Example: Precious Liz

Here's a precious example.

I have a dear friend named Liz, who three years ago became deathly ill with a "stage four" cancer. Rather than question the Lord, "Why me?," she turned it around and confessed to Him, "Why not me?"

Her radiologist told her that because the cancer was far advanced, chemo probably wood be fruitless. However, he admitted he could not deny her the chance of recovery and suggested she do chemo and radiation at the same time! This is a procedure used very rarely because it is extremely painful.

Liz was hospitalized several times and had her weekly chemo and radiation treatments at the Cancer Center, which afforded her many opportunities to witness to other patients, as well as staff. Because Liz was faithful to constantly renew her mind, "putting off" fears and doubts and anxieties, and "putting on" God's thoughts, instead, she was able to honestly tell all these people that God is real and that He loved them.

Even at one of her lowest points, when confined to the hospital, Liz asked her doctor for permission on Saturday morning to travel 50 miles to attend the *Faith in the Night Seasons* seminar. His answer was, of course, "no way!" He left the room, but returned a few moments later to ask her, "What's so important about this seminar that you insist upon going to?" It was a "God-appointed moment" where she could speak to him about faith and "night seasons." Surprisingly, he then granted her permission to go, but made her promise to go straight from the hospital to the meeting and then return straight back afterwards to her hospital bed. She agreed.

But after her first time, her doctor noticed such an excellent change in her that he gave her permission to go *every* Saturday. He told her, "You seem to get much more benefit from that seminar material than we can give you here with our I.V.'s and other treatments. You may continue to go..."

God in His sovereignty has chosen to heal Liz completely.

Today, she is a radiant example and walking testimony of God's Love and faithfulness. Everyone who knows her will attest that she's a total miracle! But, much of her healing, I believe, is due to her willingness to continually take every thought captive, deal with it and give it to God. And, because of that, the Lord faithfully continues to transform her and fill her with His life.

Recently, Liz found another suspicious lump. She had no way of knowing if it was cancerous or not. She immediately called her doctor and was told to come right in to be examined. A physician's assistant checked her and called in the doctor who scheduled surgery immediately. She went to the hospital, but when the surgeon and his team again checked her, prior to surgery, they were unable to find the lump. The surgery was canceled and she was sent home. The lump has not appeared again!

Liz told me recently, "I like to think that God has used my illness to educate and strengthen my oncologist in his profession and for me to *never give up*!"

Truly, Liz is a walking miracle! She lives what she believes!

When we choose <u>not</u> to renew our minds on a daily basis, however, either because of ignorance or hidden hurts, fears and insecurities, we quench God's Spirit in our hearts and block His Life from coming forth. And, over time, we can end up with what the Bible calls a "seared (insensitive) conscience."

A Seared Conscience

I never thought much about 1 Timothy 4:2 that speaks about a "seared conscience." But a recent situation highlighted this verse and I did some research on it. First of all, these are believers that Paul is talking about,—people in church. They are people who profess to be Christians, who lead others to Christ and who do good works, yet whose consciences all the while are insensitive, either covered with grease (Psalm 119:70) or cauterized—all because they have <u>not</u> renewed their minds nor dealt with their sin and self.

When the Holy Spirit pinpoints their sinful ways, they choose to ignore it. Thus a stronghold is created, a hideout or haven for the enemy. If this continues over a period of time their conscience will lose it's ability to hear God's voice. And, eventually, these Christians, having turned out that "still small voice," will be unable to come to repentance. They no longer feel godly sorrow. Consequently, the life that comes forth is <u>not</u> God's Life, as it should be, but their own self-life, causing them to *say* one thing and yet *do* another. Unfortunately, such 'Christians' turn many away from the Lord.

So, faith and a good conscience go together; so do hypocrisy and a bad conscience. Just as in 1 Timothy 1:5, "Now the purpose of the commandment is Love out of a pure heart, from a good conscience, and from sincere faith," so the loss of a good conscience brings about the shipwreck of our faith. Only by renewing our minds daily will we be able to walk out the above Scripture and keep us from a seared conscience.

In light of this, if we have quenched God's Spirit in our hearts by emotional choices, we should not boast about being a Christian; obviously, at that moment, we are not reflecting Him at all. Our words and our deeds don't match. We're *not living* the truth and *there's no transformed life.* The only way Christ's Life can be shown forth is by *first* "putting off" our ungodly thoughts and emotions and then "putting on" the Mind of Christ.

Why Is Mind Renewal So Important?

Having a renewed mind is absolutely critical because it's the key to our transformation! It's only as our basic thinking patterns change that our lives can change. In other words, if our basic attitudes are not renewed, then our lives will never be transformed either, no matter what we do or try.

After being a Christian for almost 50 years, I'm convinced that maturity in Christ is not just knowing a bunch of Scriptures, going to church regularly, attending prayer meetings, leading Bible studies and writing books, but simply *knowing how moment-by-moment to make the proper choices to renew our minds.* Then God's Life from our hearts can come forth and, we'll have the freedom to drop our masks and facades, be real and transparent and yet *still reflect Christ,* just as Liz did. This is the *genuine* witness, the pure heart and the good conscience that others will notice and want what we have. They did with Liz, and they will with us also!

So just because we're Christians does <u>not</u> mean we *automatically* have God's thoughts. We don't, and especially in trials. Just as God's Love can be blocked by our emotional choices, so God's thoughts can also be withheld. And, of course, in trials this becomes even more evident.

Now, there are many reasons why mind renewal is so important. Let's explore three of the major ones here:

1) Mind renewal is important because <u>God wants us to see every situation He allows into our lives from His viewpoint and His perspective</u>.

God wants us to discern everything that happens from His vantage point and His perspective. As we said before, in a difficult situation we usually "think" with our feelings. God wants us to reverse this, learn to set aside our own thoughts, and trust our situation to His wisdom.

Remember David Flood in Chapter 1 and what happened to him when his wife suddenly died? He reacted emotionally and began to doubt God. He ended up totally in despair, at the bottom of the enemy's **cycle of defeat**. If he could only have acknowledged his true feelings and given his doubt to God, the Lord would have given him peace and eventually shown him the good that would come out of his tragedy.

Isaiah 55:8 tells us that our own natural thinking is not only different from God's, it is completely opposite from God's.[15] Haven't you ever experienced this to be true? You'll just have figured out in your head how God is going to work out your circumstances, and then all of a sudden He turns around and accomplishes His will in a totally different way.

This is where God's **cycle of trust** comes in:

> "Trust in the Lord with all thine heart, and *lean not to thine own understanding.* In all thy ways acknowledge Him, and He will direct your paths." (Proverbs 3:5-6)

2)   Another reason why mind renewal is so important is because <u>whoever directs and controls our thinking, ultimately is the one who will direct and control our lives</u>.[17] There's a natural chain reaction that occurs in our souls that determines our actions. Here's how it works: what we <u>think</u> affects how we feel; how we <u>feel</u> influences our desires; and our <u>desires</u> (or our choices) produce our <u>actions</u>.

Thus, if we can catch our negative thoughts when they first occur, we'll be able to stop the whole chain reaction before it even begins. We might even be able to prevent sin before it occurs in our lives. But, if we don't take every thought captive, we end up being carried along by the tide of emotion, quenching God's Spirit, and again, self life will show forth in our souls.

Therefore, whenever a negative, self-reflective thought comes in, instantly refuse it, reject it, and crucify it. Don't give way to adverse imagination or reflection. Try to keep clearness of mind and purity of heart at all times. Don't allow negative thoughts to go unchecked to the point where you again dwell on them. Recognize these kinds of pessimistic thoughts, and immediately choose to give them to God. Making these kinds of faith choices takes the "*weighed down*" feelings away. The more we do this, the lighter we'll feel. And the reason is, God is re-aligning our negative thoughts and feelings with our faith choices.

An Example: Mother-in-law Troubles

A perfect example: Many years ago, I received a letter from a dear friend of mine, explaining a very difficult situation she'd had with her mother-in-law. Carol explained that if she hadn't known how to make "contrary choices," she could have easily ended up devastated.

This is what she wrote:

"My mother-in-law had come for a two-and-a-half week visit at Christmas time. During this time, the Lord had allowed a number of pressure points to surface in our relationship— pressures that can so easily occur, especially during the busy holiday season. The enemy continually sought to divide us.

"I had been planning to give my husband a special surprise gift for his 50th birthday coming up shortly after the holidays. In order to give him this gift, I needed to trust the Lord for two things: child care for one week for my seven-year-old daughter; and $700, which I did not have. Within one day, the Lord provided the child care.

"The day before Christmas, my mother-in-law asked what I was going to do for my husband's birthday. When I told her about the surprise, she volunteered to pay for half of it. My first response was to decline her generous offer, knowing that she was on a limited income, but since she was insistent, I believed it was the Lord's way of answering my prayer. I was still a bit uneasy about it, however.

"Later that same day, my mother-in-law came to me and said, 'Well, when are you going to tell him about his birthday gift?' Now, I had it all planned in my mind how I was going to surprise my husband on his actual birthday. When I told her this, she became very hurt, letting me know that since she was the one who was going to pay for half of it, she should be able to tell her son now, since she would not be here on his birthday.

"'Self' screamed inside, 'It's not fair! I planned this surprise! I didn't want her money anyway!' But, I knew deep within my spirit, however, that I was to do as she wished.

"I relinquished my desires to God and asked Him to give me the grace I needed. It was so exciting—God not only gave me His words to tell her this, but He also changed my feelings, softened my voice, and filled me with His Love for her.

"I knew God was in this because it was no longer important to me to have 'my way.' What became preeminent was, 'Will I choose to be and do what God wants?'

"Well, she did tell my husband, and she did spoil my surprise, but God did deliver me. He took away my hurt and disappointment, and replaced them with His Love in my heart. We ended up having a great birthday week."

Philippians 4:8 instructs us to fill our minds with good things. This means that after we have made the correct faith choices, we are to fill our minds with Godly thoughts: "Finally, brethren, whatsoever things are true, whatsoever things are honest, whatsoever things are just, whatsoever things are pure, whatsoever things are lovely, whatsoever things are of good report; if there be any virtue, and if there be any praise, think on these things."

If Satan can influence our thinking by simply keeping us immersed in our own natural, emotional way of responding, he's got us! He doesn't have to do another thing. We've played right into his hands—we're side tracked. At that point, he's the one directing our lives and, we're about ready to slide down his **cycle of defeat**.

I talked to a woman yesterday who is going through a horrendous trial. Her husband has lost his job. They are about ready to lose their home. Their marriage is extremely fragile and in crisis. She told me, "Nancy, I can't stop feeling afraid. I'm going deeper and deeper in the pit. I just feel there's no hope for us. I'm paralyzed; I feel like giving up."

The enemy has so penetrated her thinking that her actions simply followed suit. We'll talk more in just a moment about this chain reaction of our soul. The opposite is also true, however: if we allow the Lord to direct our thinking, then He will be the One who controls our lives.

3) A third reason why mind renewal is so important is that if there is no mind change, there will be no life change either.

Simply, without a renewed mind, our lives will remain unchanged. No matter how many Bible studies we attend, how many Scriptures we read, how often we go to church or how much we pray, *if we don't have a mind change, our lives will still have the same problems, the same failures, and the same defeats as they always have.*

This is why God puts such emphasis in the Bible on taking every thought captive and renewing our minds. (2 Corinthians 10:5) He knows that unless we learn to "deal" with each pain, each hurt, each insecurity, each instance of pride and unbelief as it occurs, we'll just continue to act out of these negative things, no matter what we do or what we try. Consequently, the same crumbling that has occurred all along in our lives, will just continue to happen. If there is *ever* to be any *life change* at all, there *first* needs to be a mind change.

Making Faith Choices

So what's the answer? How do we renew our minds so that we *can* break that chain reaction? The solution is simply learning how to make "faith choices" which we spoke about earlier in my illustration about Chip. Let me explain:

If we are believers, then God has given us *His* power and *His* authority to make "non-feeling choices." These are faith choices where we say "not my will, but Thine," just as Jesus did. (Matthew 26:39) As Christians, God has given us the ability to choose to go *against the tide* of our emotions and do what He has asked (*even though we really don't want to do it, don't feel like doing it or even think it won't work*). God promises to honor these choices because they open the door to His Spirit. Simply put, *faith choices activate the will in overcoming the mind and the emotions.* Thus, moment by moment, we have the free choice to choose by faith to "walk after His Spirit" and do what *He* has asked, or "walk after the flesh," doing what our *own desires* tell us. (Romans 7 and 8)

In the second choice, "self-life" rather than Christ's Life, will show forth in our lives. Unfortunately, because so many Christians don't understand this concept and continue to make emotional choices that reveal self-life rather than God's, non-believers think Christians are hypocrites. And I don't blame them. Too many of us *say* one thing with our words yet *show* something totally different in our actions. We love God emotionally and we attend church, but since we continue to make "fleshly or worldly choices," self-life continually shows forth. Interestingly enough, non-believers know the difference! And so do kids! They know when it's real and they know when it's not! So even though we proclaim Christ with our words, our actions often reveal that we are far from Him.

The sad part about all of this is that many of us know something is wrong with our walk, but we haven't the faintest idea how to fix it. I know, because I've been there!

The answer boils down to that "moment-by-moment choice" to continually renew our minds and not go by emotions.

God Changes Our Feelings

Something very important to note here is that we are not responsible to change our negative feelings. It's totally impossible to do that! We're only responsible to put in charge the One who can change our feelings and that, of course, is God. And again, the way we do this is by making non-feeling choices to renew our minds. God, then, in His perfect timing, will change our feelings and our thoughts to match the faith choices we have made. In other words, *He aligns our feelings with our choices and thus makes us genuine.*

As humans, we are so programmed to *feel* everything we choose. When we make a faith choice to do something we don't feel, we often think it's not genuine. We feel phony. However this is <u>not</u> the case in God's kingdom. Christians have the supernatural ability and power (because of the indwelling Spirit of God) to *go against* what they think and feel, because God has given us His *authority* to do so. So the authority and power is God's, but the choice is always ours.

There's a story in Mark 9:24 that validates this very principle. A father brings a demon-possessed child to Jesus and asks Him if He can help. Jesus answers that, "all things are possible to him that believeth." The father then cries out, "Lord, I believe; [now] help Thou mine unbelief." In other words, "Lord, I choose to believe by faith what You promise; now make my feelings align with that choice."

That's exactly what our response should be.

An Example: Rats, Spiders and Insects

An example of how God faithfully changes our feelings to match our choices is a dear friend of mine, Leona, who used to be a missionary in Bangkok, Thailand.

The first year she was in Thailand was absolutely miserable for her. She was allergic to much of the Thai food and would become violently ill every time she ate. Also she hated the hot, sticky, muggy weather with its huge spiders and insects and the abundance of rats and crawling vermin infesting most of the buildings.

In addition to these problems, Leona didn't know the Thai language, so she was extremely lonely. She had no friends in the country, no permanent church home, nor any person to turn to for spiritual help, encouragement or just plain fellowship.

Over and over again by faith, she chose to trust that God <u>had</u> sent her there for a reason and a purpose. She gave God her emotional feelings about her environment, rather than to be consumed by them, and determined to follow Him regardless of how she felt. In time, the Lord aligned her feelings with what she had so faithfully chosen.

What was so exciting for me then was to witness her change of heart—from the first year, where every letter related how much she hated everything that had to do with Thailand, to the recent year when she visited us and I heard her say, "I can't wait to get home to Thailand. I miss my friends, the food and, yes, even the bugs and the weather."

We Must Be Believers

Before we go any further, it's critical to understand that unless we have asked Christ into our hearts to be our Savior and have been *born again* by His Spirit, we'll be unable to make these kinds of faith choices. Consequently, in order to *put off* our sin and self and *put on* Christ, we must *first* have a brand-new spirit within us that *will* produce something different from what we naturally think, feel and want to do. John 3:5-6 validates this: "Except a man be born of water and of the Spirit, he cannot enter into the kingdom of God. That which is born of the flesh is flesh; and that which is born of the Spirit is spirit."

Simply put, this means that those who don't possess the Spirit of God in their hearts cannot make non-feeling choices, because they don't possess a Power Source within them to perform what they, in themselves, cannot. Believers—indwelt by the Holy Spirit however, do!

A Christian with Christ's Spirit dwelling in his heart has *God's* authority and *God's* power to override his negative thoughts and feelings, and to say like Jesus, "not my will, but Thine." (Matthew 26:39) God, then, in His timing and in His way, will not only align this person's feelings with what he has chosen by faith, He will also give him the *power* to accomplish that will in his life.

Practical Steps to Renewing our Minds

Before we go on and list the practical steps to renewing our minds daily, I want to first encourage you to heed 2 Corinthians 10:5-6 which says that we are to be zealous in "Casting down imaginations and every high thing that exalteth itself against the knowledge of God, and *bringing into captivity every thought to the obedience of Christ*; and *being ready to revenge all disobedience*, when your obedience is fulfilled."

Now, when God says *take every thought captive*, He obviously doesn't mean examine every single thought that we have. He means to stop and take a good, hard look at the anxious thoughts, the hurtful ones, the doubtful ones, the frustrations, the anger, the pride, and all the other "emotional" and self-centered thoughts that take away our peace. *Lack of peace is a good barometer to see which thoughts God wants us to deal with*. Romans 14:23 teaches that "whatever is not of faith is sin." So any thought that is *not of faith* and that takes away our peace is a thought we must deal with.

Most of us have not really considered doing this before. We've just reacted naturally, even after becoming Christians. Most of the time we don't stop and think before we respond. We just do what comes naturally. And, herein lies the problem... Learn to *filter* every thought and you will be amazed to learn what you are really thinking!

What happens when we *don't* take every thought captive, is that we go with the flow of emotion—that chain reaction—and, quite often, end up in the devil's **cycle of defeat**—confused, discouraged, and depressed. This, of course, is exactly what the enemy wants. What we have forgotten to do is make the necessary faith choices to renew our minds—to put off the junk and put on Christ.

All this takes constant discipline and effort. But what happens when we give into our unruly emotions is that we spiral right down into the enemy's pit! *If we don't take our ungodly thoughts captive, they end up taking us captive*!

The following four essential steps to renewing our minds daily are based upon the four steps that the priests of Solomon's Temple went through in order to be cleansed and reconciled with God.

Recognize Self-Centered Thoughts

1) The first step we must take in order to renew our minds daily is to <u>recognize, acknowledge and experience the negative thoughts and emotions</u> that have just occurred.

We're not to *vent* these things nor *push them down* into the hidden part of our soul, but simply ask the Lord to expose what's *really* going on inside us. This is the time that it's important to get alone with the Lord so we can go through these steps and deal with our sin properly. Try not to put this off. Every time I put off going through these steps, I contaminate everyone I come in contact with! As Isaiah 3:24 tells us, "Instead of [a] sweet smell there shall be [a] stink."

Therefore, whenever I find myself hurt, angry, resentful, critical, self-centered, prideful, ungrateful, anxious, afraid, confused, bitter, judgmental, or filled with <u>any</u> negative emotion, I call time-out, get alone with God and go through these steps. Jesus is the only One who can expose and cleanse my sin and heal me from the inside out.

We must understand that we are *not* responsible for the original, negative thought when it first comes into our thinking. That's not the sin. It's what we choose to do with that thought that produces the sin or not. If we recognize that ungodly thought and choose to give it over to God, then we have not sinned and we have not quenched His Spirit. However, if we do nothing with that thought, but allow it to fester our self-centered emotions, then, of course, it will be sin and it will quench His Spirit in us.

It's important to understand that we cannot hold on to these thoughts or feelings without eventually acting out of them. Even if we try to keep them buried, they still will become the motivation for much of our future actions, whether we are aware of it or not. Burying our hurts, memories, and fears does not get rid of them. Only allowing God to expose them and giving them to Him, does.

We are to ask Him not only to expose what's going on in our conscious thoughts and emotions—things that we can see, but we also must ask Him to shed light on the *hidden things* in our soul—the things we cannot see.

The surface emotions can often be just the *symptoms* of a much deeper cause. If the real root problem can be exposed, and subsequently gotten rid of, then the surface emotions will not occur again either. If, however, we only deal with the external emotions and never the root cause, the surface problems will come again and again and again. This makes it essential that we always ask the Lord to expose root causes.

Scripture never says that we won't have negative or self-centered thoughts, emotions and desires.[17] We will. We're still human and we'll have these kinds of thoughts and feelings until the day we see Jesus. The Bible does say, however, that we can have victory over the "desires of the flesh,"[18] if we constantly make faith choices.

Confess and Repent

2) The next step to renewing our minds is to confess and repent of all that the Holy Spirit has shown us and, in addition, unconditionally forgive anyone who has wronged us.

Confession simply means taking responsibility for our negative thoughts and emotions and acknowledging that what we have thought or done has quenched God's Spirit in us. Because it's sin, we must therefore confess ownership of it.

Repenting is simply choosing to turn away from these things that separate us from God in order to choose, in obedience, to follow what He wants of us.

This critical step of confession and repentance is our *own responsibility*. (As 1 John 1:9 says, "If *we* confess our sins, *He* is faithful and just to forgive us our sins.") It is the step that too often many of us leave out when we give things to the Lord. Most of us are willing to relinquish our hurts, fears and doubts to God but often <u>un</u>willing to admit our own responsibility in them. This is the reason why so many of the things we give to God seem to come back and back and back. We've omitted personal confession and repentance!

An example is depression. If we are depressed (and I am assuming that the depression is emotionally and mentally caused, and not physiologically induced), and we have been following this emotional way of thinking for some time, we cannot simply say to the Lord, "Help me with my depression," and expect Him to take it away automatically.

Rather, we must say, "Father, I *confess* I am depressed (I *own* these emotions). I confess I have chosen to entertain and follow these morose feelings over what You would have me do and it has quenched Your Spirit in me. It's sin. I now choose to turn around (I *repent)* from following what these things are telling me and choose, instead, to follow You and what You want me to do."

Again, remember we're not responsible to change our feelings. We can't do that. We are only responsible to put in charge the Person who *can* change our feelings and that's God. And, again, we do this by confessing we *own* the feelings and then repenting of them. God then will be free to change our feelings and align them with our faith choices.

Forgive Others

A part of this second step is that we must also **unconditionally forgive** anyone else involved for whatever things done to us. Unforgiveness is one of the many attitudes that quench God's Spirit in us. And, if we hold on to it, it will hinder God from working *in* us and *through* us. Therefore, the way we release God to work in our situations is by unconditionally forgiving, whether the other party has asked for it or not!

Don't misunderstand, we are <u>not</u> pardoning these people. We don't have the authority or the right to do that. That's God's responsibility. When we unconditionally forgive, we are simply releasing them to God so that <u>He,</u> then, can judge them righteously, and also so that our response to their sin won't become a stumbling block in us.

We choose to forgive them because we are commanded to do so by Jesus. Mark 11:25-26 says, "And when ye stand praying, forgive, if ye have anything against any, that your Father also, who is in heaven, may forgive you your trespasses. *But if ye do not forgive, neither will your Father, who is in heaven, forgive your trespasses.*"[19] (See also Matthew 6:14-15) It is necessary that we forgive others so that He can forgive us.

Sometimes, especially in trials, it's very difficult to forgive others for their part. But this is just another place that we can give God our "justified" feelings and trust Him for His *unconditional* Love for those other people. 2 Corinthians 2:10 tells us, it's only through Jesus and what He has done for us that we can extend unconditional forgiveness. If this is a stumbling block for you, put a marker here and skip to Chapter 7, where there are some incredible examples of unconditional forgiveness.

Give All to the Lord

3) Once God has revealed our ungodly thoughts and emotions and we have confessed our responsibility in them, the next essential step is to <u>give them over to Him</u>.

God will not violate our free will by forcibly taking these things from us; we must willingly sacrifice them into His hands. We must not only give Him our fears, resentments and unforgiveness, but also our confusion, dismay and disappointments.

We are told in Romans 12:1 that we must present our bodies to the Lord as a "living sacrifice." In other words, God wants us to sacrifice, or give to Him, everything that is not of faith, so that it can be purged and cleansed by His Blood. When we willingly give Him our sin and our self, He promises to take it as "far as the east is from the west." (Psalm 103:12)

Do we trust God enough to do this continually? Can we leave not only our most prized possessions at the altar—our families and loved ones—but also our worries, confusion and discouragement? That's the question.

Strongholds of the Enemy

Now, most of the things we give to the Lord will be "of the flesh" and will usually go away immediately or at least within a few days, if we are faithful to go through the above cleansing steps. However, some of the things that the Lord might expose will be long-standing strongholds of the enemy, and he won't let these things go easily. So don't be dismayed if certain thoughts and feelings seem to reappear even after you have given them to God.

If things do seem to come back, don't give up and say, "Oh, this just doesn't work for me!" That's exactly what the enemy wants you to do. He wants you to give up. The truth is that the Lord takes our negative thoughts the moment we give them to Him, but often *our feelings won't align with that faith choice for awhile.* And this is where Satan tries to make us think that God is not faithful and that He has not taken our sins away. Satan wants to use these 'in-between' times—between the time we give our self to God and the time the Lord finally aligns our feelings with our choices—to deceive us. <u>God</u>, on the other hand, lets us go awhile to test us, strengthen our faith and our love.

So, recognize it's a battle. Know you will win if you will just persevere. God is already the victor. Luke 10:19 assures us that we have authority over all the power of the enemy. Recognize, however, that it might take some time before you will *see* and *feel* that victory.

It's important to do something "physical" with the things that you give over to the Lord, in order to truly experience getting rid of them. A dear friend of mine writes down on a scrap of paper all her hurts, wounds, memories: whatever God has shown her. Then she literally wraps these pieces of paper up in packages and presents them to God as "love gifts."

Personally, I like to burn them! I write down everything I give to God (all the big things) and then burn those scraps of paper. I like to watch them being consumed. To me, it's a graphic picture that those things will never come back. They are gone forever.

Read His Word

4) The final step in renewing our mind is that we must now read God's Word and replace the enemy's lies with His Truth.

Only God can *cleanse, sanctify and heal our souls completely.* And He does so by His Word. Nothing soothes or gives us as much hope, especially in trials, as hearing God's comforting voice through His Word.

After going through these four steps, then—just like the priests in Solomon's temple—we feel "bloody" and "torn apart." At this point, we are in desperate need of God's complete healing power. Only He can wash us "with the washing of water by the Word." (Ephesians 5:26)

As an aside, Dietrich Bonhoeffer once said that he never read the Bible without asking what it was really telling him to do, right then, right there, wherever he was.[20]

This is why it's helpful to memorize appropriate Scriptures, so that if we find ourselves without our Bibles, we can still lean on the Word of God. Scriptures like Psalm 32:5; all of Psalm 51; 1 John 1:5-10; Galatians 2:20 and 2 Corinthians 7:1 are vital to have ready in our memory banks.

After we have done these steps (acknowledged our self-serving sin, confessed it, repented of it and given it to God, we can be assured that we have *put off* our sin and self and *put on* His Mind. We can now step out in confident faith.

You also might try keeping a daily journal of all you give to the Lord. This will help keep you accountable.

By writing down these things, *sin* and *self* will not be able to accumulate. In other words, you won't be able to go on to the issues of tomorrow if you haven't first dealt with the situations of today. Writing things down will help you keep very short lists.

Praise and Worship

After we have done these four steps of renewing our minds, we can now boldly enter the Lord's presence and worship Him in the "beauty of holiness." (1 Chronicles 16:29; Psalm 96:7-9; 29:2) In Hebrews Chapter 10, our encouragement is for "*boldness to enter into the Holiest* by the blood of Jesus...Let us draw near with a true heart in full assurance of faith, having our hearts sprinkled from an evil conscience, and our bodies washed with pure water." (Verses 19 & 22)

In other words, sin and self, for the time being, have been taken care of. Our hearts have been cleansed and our minds renewed, so that we now *can* enter His presence and worship Him in the same nature as He—in the spirit. This is what John means when he says "the true worshippers will worship in spirit and truth." (John 4:23-24)

Now is the time we can fill our minds with praise. Praise for who He is. Praise that He "will work all things together" for our best.[21] (See Romans 8:28) Especially during our trials, praise is what keeps our hearts and minds stayed upon Him. Try praising Him five times a day as David tells us in Psalm 119:164 that he did. It will help to keep our minds clear and focused upon Him.

[You know it's so easy for us to say, "Well, just give it to God." But, exactly *how* do we do that? Our little book *The Key: Let Go and Let God* explores the practical steps of giving things over to the Lord in a little more detail than we had room here. *How* do we take every thought captive? *How* do we confess and repent of things? And *how* do we literally give things to God?]

Conclusion

Going through these steps of renewing our minds every time we are confronted with depression, fear, confusion, doubt, insecurity, discouragement, or *whatever* is not of faith, is the only way we can stay open and cleansed vessels so that God can continue to form Christ in us. It's also the surest way to avoid falling into the enemy's **cycle of defeat**.

God wants us freed! He wants us freed from ourselves, freed from others' responses, freed from our circumstances and freed from Satan's deceptions. It is a renewed mind that gives us this wonderful freedom.

Transformation into Christ's image is God's will for each of us. And we implement His will through *first,* knowing He loves us then unconditionally obeying Him (by learning to love Him, by learning to renew our minds and, by learning to have unshakeable faith). He wants us living the Truth so that our words and deeds match. As we have seen, the only way this is possible is by the constant renewing of our minds— the setting aside of our own natural, emotional way of thinking and beginning to think with the Mind of Christ.

Never is this more important than when we are in the midst of a crisis—in the very eye of the storm. Never are our thoughts more desperate, our feelings more volatile and our desires more heightened! Learning how to renew our minds is, at this time, absolutely essential if we want to live God's **cycle of trust** enabling us to patiently endure what God has allowed.

"Therefore, I beseech you brethren, by the mercies of God, that ye present your bodies a living sacrifice, holy, acceptable unto God, which is your reasonable service. And, *be not conformed* to this world; but *be ye transformed by the renewing of your mind*, that ye may prove what is that good and acceptable and perfect will of God." (Romans 12:1-2)

(If you are interested in studying further how we renew our minds and how we put on the Mind of Christ, be sure to see *Be Ye Transformed*. It's a fascinating study, likening the architecture of our body, soul and spirit to the layout and design of Solomon's Temple. These comprise the Outer Court, Inner Court and Holy Place. The secret, hidden chambers of the temple where the priests stored their own idolatrous worship items are compared to our own innermost part where we hide and bury our hurts, unforgiveness and bitterness. God has given us a perfect Scriptural model or pattern to help understand what happens when we block or quench God's Spirit, and, what we look like when filled with His Spirit.)

"**He staggered not at the promise of God through unbelief, but was strong in faith, giving glory to God, and** *being fully persuaded that what He had promised He was able also to perform.*" **(Romans 4:20)**

Chapter 5
In Obedience: Learning to Have Unshakeable Faith

Over the last several chapters we have seen how God's **cycle of trust** works and how critical it is to know His will and His Love. This will give us the confidence to obey Him in all things, enable us to "see" Him and have the ability to persevere through all the events He allows. But trust, as we are beginning to understand, is the critical ingredient when we face trials, tribulations and tragedies. Without trust, we cannot obey; we cannot love; and we certainly cannot have faith.

In the previous chapters, we explored the first two essentials keys of obedience: learning to love God more and learning to renew our minds on a moment-by-moment basis. The third key of obedience, which we want to study here, is learning how to have unconditional faith.

Few subjects in the Bible are more important for us to understand than that of *faith*. Yes, "loving God" is critical. That's basic. Yes, "renewing our mind" is essential. It's the place that the battle is fought. But choosing to have "unconditional faith" in God during a trial is absolutely vital. If we lose our faith, then *everything* else shuts down.

Naked faith—unconditional faith—is being *convinced* that no matter what <u>we</u> see, hear, feel or think, <u>God</u> will keep His Word and do the impossible. It's believing that God will do whatever He has promised to do, even though we might not understand how. Again, Job 13:15 gives the proper faith response: "Though You slay me, *yet will I trust You.*"

Another response of unconditional faith in the Lord is found in Romans 4:21 where Paul speaks of being "*fully persuaded* that what He had promised, He was able also to perform." (Bear with me if I use this Scripture a lot. It's one of my life verses. Naked faith is choosing to believe that God will do whatever He promises, regardless of what we see, hear, feel or think. Naked faith means radical reliance upon God. It's not feeling, not seeing, not understanding and not knowing *but trusting God anyway.* It's being convinced that regardless of what we see happening before our eyes, regardless of what we understand to be true, and regardless of how we feel, *God will be faithful to His Word and perform His promises in His timing and in His way!* This is the only kind of faith that will get us through.

Some of us, however, will never advance to this stage, because we'll grow impatient in our crises and seek our own solution. Only naked faith will allow us to endure to the end, never give up and never turn back.

The Testing of Our Faith

Everywhere we look today, our Christian faith is being tested. Whether it's through crumbling marriages, financial difficulties, family problems, serious illness, the death of a loved one or business-related problems, our faith seems to be in the crucible!

1 Peter 4:17 tells us that as God begins to wrap up time as we know it, He's going to allow events to occur in the Body of Christ that will try us to the extreme. As we said in the Introduction, "judgment begins at

the house of God." Thus, it's imperative that we have a grasp of what real faith is and, most importantly, understand what real faith would have us to do. Otherwise, how will we make it through the coming time of testing just prior to Jesus' return?

God is teaching us to believe in, act upon and walk out His promises *by faith*. And, even if we might not see His promises being fulfilled in the way we "thought" they would, He still calls us to believe. Naked faith is allowing God to do in our lives all that is necessary—whether it's appearance is happy or hard— in order to conform us more into His image. Naked faith is simply the *unequivocal strong conviction that no matter what happens, God will never leave us or forsake us.*

An Example: Lyn

I met Lyn a number of years ago on one of our trips overseas. When I heard her testimony, I was astounded at all that God had allowed in her life. One wonders just how much a person can take. I asked Lyn to write me her story. Here's a portion of what she had to say:

"In coming to Australia, I thought that being prepared to accept the loss of my marriage, children, and other family members, friends, home, security, our business, the loss of my reputation, the church I attended, and leaving the country I loved to go to a country where I knew no one, was giving God 'everything.' On top of all that, I no longer had a job or finances, due to my health.

"Even though I was reading every book I could get my hands on concerning dying to self, I lost all hope and found myself on the verge of a breakdown. I was angry. Very angry with God. Deeply depressed and often suicidal. I am ashamed to say that after calling myself a Christian for 30 years, I still did not trust Him enough to make the right decisions.

"Finally, after many months in this state, I said, 'Okay, have it Your way! I truly give You everything...my fears, my mind, my will and my obedience, and I choose to live out of Your strength, not my own.' I chose at that moment to stop believing the lies that Satan had been telling me about myself and made the choice to put God first in everything.

"As a result of that commitment and that choice, my life changed drastically. It's not back to where I want it yet, but I have peace and I am content. God has heard me."

Faith Is Not a Feeling

The predicament that many of us find ourselves in, is that we have wrongly chosen to associate our faith with our feelings. This kind of *emotional faith* can only survive as long as life is understandable and within our "control." But what happens when the rug of human understanding is pulled out from under us and events in our lives turn chaotic and uncontrollable? We'll sink, because our faith is built on emotionalism and <u>not</u> on the solid rock of faith in Christ. It's called "spiritual vertigo."

Chuck tells me that as a pilot it's very important to continually rely upon your "cross check" list, especially when flying in rough weather. Your altitude, rate of climb, air speed, attitude indicator, compass heading and your turn and bank indicator are all essential components of a safe flight. If you focus on any <u>one</u> of these, and not the others, you'll end up in trouble. Well, it's the same with our faith. We mustn't let it be based on one facet—only our emotions. It must be built upon <u>all</u> the components that make up faith, predominately obedience, trust and love, in order that we continue to walk in the midst of the storms and in order to avoid "spiritual vertigo."

Faith is <u>not</u> a feeling: it's simply the power to believe, and the ability to see everything that happens to us, through God's eyes. It's being able to keep afloat in the dark sea of overwhelming circumstances. Only through this kind of pure faith will everything eventually be turned to sight and understanding, and we'll finally be able to move out from our familiar comfort zone into the realm of the unknown.

Hebrews 11 is a powerful chronicle of those who, by listening to and obeying the voice of the Lord, stepped unquestionably out into the unknown. It says: *by faith* Noah prepared an ark...*by faith* Abraham went out...*by faith* Sarah received the ability to conceive...*by faith* Moses kept the Passover...*by faith* the people of God passed through the Red Sea...*by faith* the walls of Jericho fell down...and *by faith* Rahab the harlot did not perish.

When we study the lives of the above saints, we quickly understand that faith is not something <u>we</u> hold onto but rather *Someone who holds onto us!* True faith steps out of the crowd that's still clamoring for understanding, lays itself humbly at the foot of the Cross and whispers, "Though You slay me, yet will I trust You."

True faith is trusting that God loves us and that He will work out every detail of our lives for His glory, even if our *senses are screaming just the opposite.*

The fact remains that *our faith is never more alive than when what we are experiencing in our spirit contradicts what our senses are saying.*

A Perfect Example: "A Gift from God"

Captain Eddie Rickenbacker, the winner of the Congressional Medal of Honor, is well known in military circles for his daring exploits as a World War I flying ace. What is not known about him is an incident in World War II that led to his public declaration of faith.

In October 1942, he was on a special mission for the Secretary of War. As he was leaving California in a B17 to deliver a secret message to General Douglas MacArthur, the plane's tire blew out. Repairs were made, but what no one knew was that the accident had disturbed the plane's sensitive navigational instruments. So, unbeknown to anyone, the "damaged" plane took off for the long trip to Canton Island where MacArthur was stationed. As they approached the place where the island was supposed to be, they saw no island and no land, only miles and miles of blue ocean. The aircraft circled, desperately trying to find a landing site, but finally ran out of fuel and crashed.

All eight men aboard the plane climbed into three small life rafts. They roped themselves together, but were without any food or water. They survived for eight full days with only a few oranges and Rickenbacker's copy of the New Testament. Every morning and evening, he insisted upon reading a few chapters and praying. At first there were objections. But as the days went on and the hardships became intolerable, they asked him to pray and read more.

On the eighth day, Rickenbacker, dazed and near death, felt something land on his head. Instinctively he knew it was a seagull. Very slowly, he reached up and grabbed it. That "gift from God" began the steps of survival that would otherwise have been impossible. God had heard their heartfelt prayers and had answered them. They divided the bird among themselves, used its innards for bait to catch fish, and survived 16 more days until rescued.

Eddie Rickenbacker was convinced that God had heard his spirit-led prayers, sent him a special love gift and kept him alive so that he could serve Him for the rest of his life.[22]

Remember, the presence of God can *only* be seen through faith, not through our own understanding. Only by faith, can we recognize Him in every circumstance; only by faith, can we know His closeness; and only by faith, can we please Him in all we do.

The question is: Can we step out in this kind of faith?

Enemy's Cycle of Defeat vs. God's Cycle of Trust

During our trials, tribulations and tragedies, because we will be experiencing such a wide variety of emotions, it's vitally important to be honest with ourselves and express exactly what we are feeling. As we mentioned last chapter, taking every thought captive and acknowledging our real thinking and feelings is the first step to renewing our minds.

Some of the more common emotions we'll be experiencing are discouragement, confusion and depression. Remember, these are some of the first emotions that makeup the enemy's **cycle of defeat**: *discouragement* leads to *confusion*; confusion develops into *depression*; and depression results in *loss of vision, disorientation, despair* and, finally, *defeat*—the feeling of totally giving up.

Let's delve into these three emotional states of mind—discouragement, confusion and depression— for just a moment, so we can recognize them, deal with them and learn to have the faith to overcome them. Remember, if we don't recognize these when they first occur, they will start that "chain reaction" within our soul that will eventually produce our actions.

Discouragement

Discouragement is an emotion that every single one of us has, at one time or another experienced. In fact, it's one of the first emotions we'll encounter during difficult times, especially if events have turned out worse than we expected.

Discouragement is simply disappointed hope. It's the feeling that 'because God didn't do what He promised, He really doesn't care. If He cared for me, He would have done... this... or that' (our own desires and plans). There's a deep bitterness that arises from within us that cries out like Job 3:25, "For the thing which I greatly feared is come upon me."

I remember feeling this way after Chip died.

In the meantime, we go on and live life as normally as we possibly can. However, when we read the Word, we don't get the satisfaction from it that we used to. We try to pray, but all our spiritual feelings are gone. We go to our special Bible studies, but only get very little out of them. Even when we run to hear our favorite speakers or listen to inspirational worship music, nothing moves our hearts as it once did. All our old ways of edifying ourselves don't seem to work any longer. There seems to be a grey cloud that hangs over us that just won't go away; it's dark and black and it continues to take away our hope. *It's called discouragement, an emotion we've all encountered at some point, and must recognize and deal with.*

If we let discouragement stick around, it makes us feel as if we have "lost" God and that we're no longer "special" to Him.[23] It makes us want to give up and let go.

The truth is, of course, that God never takes His eyes off of us...even for a moment. He's not missing; He's where we least expect Him. He is in the trial![24]

God never leads us into a situation only to abandon us there. That's not His way. That's not His character. In Hebrews 13:5 Jesus promises us, "*I will never leave thee, nor forsake thee.*" But, for this short period of time, He has allowed these difficult circumstances in our lives to test our faith and bring us into an intimacy with Him that we have never before experienced. He has allowed this trial to strengthen us and grow us up even more. Our expectations and hopes were for something else, but He knew exactly what we needed to be stretched and changed. And, thus, we need to lay even our hopes and expectations on the altar.

So, watch out for discouragement! We're all human and it's natural to feel this way at times. However, just don't stay there. Deal with it. Go through the steps of renewing your mind that you learned last chapter, and choose by faith to trust God anyway. Then, learn how to truly worship the Lord in the privacy of your home. Scripture tells us that "only in His presence is there fulness of joy." Learning to worship Him turns our discouragement into the joy of His presence.

If you don't *choose by faith* to do these three things—love Him, renew your mind and have unconditional trust—you'll be one step down the ladder to the enemy's trap.

An Example: Elijah

Whenever I think of discouragement and the feeling of wanting to give up, I immediately remember the story of Elijah, which begins in 1 Kings 17.

As you recall, Elijah magnificently defeated the prophets of Baal on Mt. Carmel concerning whether his God or their gods would bring rain. Elijah shouted at the prophets, "Call on the name of your gods, and I will call on the Name of the Lord; and the *God who answers by fire, let him be God.*" The prophets of Baal tried everything they could think of to get Baal to answer, but, predictably had no response. Elijah, on the other hand, summoned the fire of God which came down mightily, and eventually the rain fell.

Elijah then tried to outrun King Ahab back to the city of Jezreel because he was afraid of Ahab's wife, Jezebel. Unfortunately, he didn't make it. Jezebel was furious about the encounter on Mt. Carmel and so she sent Elijah a message that she wanted him killed. Thus, the strong, bold and brazen prophet of God on Mt. Carmel became this fearful and terrified old man who wanted to flee for his life. He found a tree (the "flesh" always seeks its own protection and covering) and, believe it or not, this mighty man of God prayed to die. He literally gave up! (1 Kings 19:3-4)

How quickly we can slide down the enemy's **cycle of defeat**.

God, however, never gives up on us. He sent an angel to tell Elijah to get up and travel to Mt. Sinai. But, on the way Elijah, again, became so discouraged that he found a cave and hid. (1 Kings 19:7-10) Can you believe it? This mighty prophet of God who just a short while ago, had called down the fire of God, is now so afraid that he is hiding in a cave! Can you relate? It's not hard to see that we are *all* built alike. We all have times of fear and insecurity and doubt. If Elijah, one of the great saints of the Old Testament knew fear, then we can expect we will also.

At this point, the Lord comes along and questions Elijah. "What are you doing here?" Elijah is so filled with self-pity, discouragement, confusion and depression that he tries to justify his position. God gently whispers to him to get up, go to Damascus and give his mantle to Elisha. What a sad ending for such a great man, because the Lord was going to remove his symbol of anointing and give it to another. Clearly, this shows how failure of faith can lead to discouragement, confusion, depression, and finally, loss of vision, despair and the feeling of wanting to give up.

In my almost 50 years of walking with the Lord I've seen this happen many times. I've seen truly gifted and anointed men of God get so discouraged, so blinded and so disoriented in their situations that God finally removed them from the empowering of His Spirit. What a tragic ending. This validates all the more the importance of "enduring and persevering to the end."

So watch out for discouragement. It's the second step into the enemy's **cycle of defeat** and the exact opposite of knowing God's Love in His **cycle of trust**.

Confusion

Discouragement often leads to confusion. And, confusion occurs because our own *expectations were not met* (at least, not met in the way we had hoped). And if we haven't dealt with our discouragement by renewing our minds, overwhelming confusion *will* result, as in the case of Elijah.

Not understanding what is happening, why it's happening and *why it contradicts what we thought the Lord told us*, is one of the hardest things to endure. Again, as in the case with Elijah, it can become totally overwhelming and frightening, especially if what's happened seems completely opposite to what the Scriptures we have received said! And so we question: "if God is with us and He promised us victory, then *why* is all this happening?[25] Is this situation from God or is it from the enemy? And why on earth am I being tested so severely?" Again, we think of Elijah's example.

Making things even worse, everything we do seems to produce even more confusion and chaos as God continues to delay all our hopes and plans and dreams. We go from the heights of expectation to the depths of despair. As Alan Redpath once expressed it, "The depths of despair to which I sank were beyond description. Sometimes I spent hours each day weeping..."[26]

The enemy, of course, is always right there whispering in our ear, telling us, "If you didn't hear God correctly this time, *you probably never do!*" And this leads us to the thought, "Since God didn't perform His promises to me here, then I can't trust the rest of His Word either." And after a while we begin to believe these things.

One woman called last week and said, "Nancy, I feel like I've been betrayed. God promised He would be with me this weekend when I went to visit my unbelieving family. I had all my church praying for me and I was totally in the Spirit when I left, but, Nancy, it went absolutely terrible. It could not have gone worse. Where was God in all of this? What about His promises to me? If I didn't hear God's Word correctly, then I must never hear Him. I feel absolutely betrayed!"

Remember, the first step on the enemy's **cycle of defeat** is doubt! And unless we recognize it, by the time confusion sets in we're already three rungs down and probably too far to stop.

An Example: Cindy

Here's a perfect example:

Remember the beautiful young woman we mentioned in the Introduction, Cindy, who has had 30 heart surgeries in the past three years?

Well, just two months ago, she went back east for a brand new experimental procedure where they attach new arteries in the places where the old ones have become clogged. Cindy was so excited to go and have the procedure done. And when she began to experience the new arteries giving her strength and vitality that she had not felt for months, she was ecstatic. She came to our ministry and enthusiastically shared how she was able, for the first time in over two years, to shovel snow off her sidewalk. This was a huge achievement for her. She was so sure that God was going to heal her that she offered to become a poster child for this new artery procedure. She was convinced that God would not have taken her this far, only to let her get sick again.

But two weeks later she again found out that her main arteries were 98% clogged.

Now, obviously, she was very confused, as any of us would be. What was God thinking of! What was He doing? She could not reason it out in her own mind. Nor could any of us who had been praying for, and watching, this beautiful child of God.

A year after being sick, yet still surviving 10 heart procedures and an open heart surgery that nearly brought death, God spoke these words to her: "*I cannot heal you until you are ready to accept how I choose to heal you. I am not finished yet!*" This personal, loving affirmation of how close God is to her, and how much He loves her keeps her strong. It wasn't a promise to heal her as she would have liked, but it *was* a promise that He sees her, cares for her and is orchestrating the entire process.

Cindy identified with the story of Hagar, an Egyptian handmaid of Sara and Abraham. Hagar was used by Sara to bear a son to her and Abraham. But afterwards Sara despised Hagar with a burning jealousy. Fleeing the wrath of her mistress, Hagar was visited by an angel of the Lord who promised her protection. Genesis 16:7 states that "the angel of the Lord found her by a fountain of water in the wilderness." Hagar then named this well of living water, Beer-lahai-roi, which means "the well of the living One seeing me."

Even though nothing made any sense to Cindy, she chose by faith to trust that God loved her, that He knew exactly what was occurring in her life and that He had everything under His control. This is where those "faith choices" must come in. *When what we see makes no sense, when it's the opposite of what we had hoped for, and when it's a blow to all our expectations, that's when we must choose by faith to trust God's hand anyway.* This is where we must choose by faith to love Him more and to renew our minds.

And, this is exactly what precious Cindy chose to do. When discouragement and confusion came over her, she acknowledged it, confessed it, repented of it and gave it to the Lord. The three anchors that the Lord gave Cindy were:

1) "<u>Beware of turning to evil</u>, which you seem to prefer to affliction..." (Job 36:21)

2) "<u>Do not grieve</u>, for the joy of the Lord is your strength." (Nehemiah 8:10b)

3) "<u>Deal courageously</u>, and the Lord shall be with the good." (2 Chronicles 19:11b; the three above quotes are from Cindy's own NIV translation)

As a result, in the middle of the trial she was able to make incredible comments like: "Well, my doctor doesn't know how much more my heart can take, *but look how much it's taken already*; and," she quipped, "since I am already *technically* dead (her heart stopped beating altogether and a pacemaker was put in), *I think I'm going to put a claim in to my insurance company. I should be eligible for the money, don't you think!*"

Now that's naked faith! Able even to kid about it, her attitude was hopeful and trusting.

Precious Cindy is a jewel in the Lord's hands. Everyone who comes into contact with her sees her trust, her obedience and her faith in the Lord, and are encouraged in their own walks with Him. Cindy has learned what it means to put her doubt, discouragement and confusion at the foot of the Cross and replace these with naked faith.

Her personal Psalm is: "I have set the Lord always before me, Because He is at my right hand, I will not be shaken. Therefore my heart is glad and my tongue rejoices; my body also will rest secure, because You will not abandon me to the grave, nor will You let your Holy One see decay. You have made known to me the path of life; You will fill me with joy in Your presence, with eternal pleasures at Your right hand." (Again from Cindy's own NIV Bible)

Our only hope for victory is to choose by faith to totally relinquish ourselves to God, permitting the crucifying process to continue. Remember Cindy. Pray for her. If she can have naked faith in her trial and not succumb to the enemy's **cycle of defeat**, then so can each one of us!

No matter what occurs, God has a wonderful plan for our lives. Thus, we must allow Him to complete what He started. He alone knows what is best for us; what He is doing; and why. Naked faith is the only answer, the only remedy and the only solution to doubt, disappointment and confusion.

Depression

The next tool in Satan's **cycle of defeat** is depression, which then leads to loss of vision, disorientation, despair and defeat—the feeling of totally giving up. Depression is rampant in the Christian Body.

Because many believers cannot bring themselves to make 'faith choices' when their worlds cave in, disappointment and confusion take over and they end up turning back. They have found the road is just too hard, too narrow and too painful to keep going. Thus, because they have <u>not</u> dealt with the previous disappointing events or the confusion that resulted, depression has set in 'big time.'

How many of us, at one time or another, have found ourselves here? I know I have. We feel paralyzed in a state of total numbness and lifelessness, as if in a dark dungeon. We just want to let go of everything and die. It's called depression.

Now, remember when we 'toy' with this state of mind, we give the enemy an even bigger entrance into our souls. Satan is a liar, a deceiver and a counterfeit. He comes to kill, steal and destroy. He comes to us not only to discourage and confuse us, but also to push us to totally give up. "It's not worth it! Let go, just give up." I can almost hear his taunts. This is one of the definitions of depression: *immobilization resulting in isolation.* It's the feeling of not wanting to try anymore, not wanting to choose anymore, not wanting to do anything at all anymore! Just give up! This is Satan's game plan: to get us *so* discouraged and *so* confused and *so* dismayed, that we actually give up and fall back! This is the enemy's objective in all of our lives.

Again, instead of implicitly trusting in God's Word, surrendering ourselves to the Holy Spirit and renewing our minds, we begin to doubt. We begin to doubt that we ever really heard God. We doubt He's really there, and, finally, we doubt that He's even real. Instead of walking by faith and making non-feeling choices, we become consumed by our emotions. And as a result, we become captive. We've fallen to the bottom of the **cycle of defeat**. Doubt in God's promises or faithfulness will affect everything we think, say and do. This, again, is his game plan. If he can convince us that God is not trustworthy, then he's got us! Because where else do we go for help? Who else has the answers to life? No one!

The only way to overcome depression, as we learned last chapter, is to make faith choices to confess it, repent of it and give it to God. God, then, in His timing will align our feelings with the choices we have made, and we can, once again, climb God's **cycle of trust**.

An Example: Joseph

Joseph is a great example of this very thing. When he was 17 years old, he received some incredible promises from God. (Genesis 37) But 13 years went by and, *instead of blessings*, Joseph was ridiculed by his family, betrayed by his brothers, and, finally, imprisoned by Potiphar (an officer of Pharaoh), with no hope of release. It seemed as if things just kept getting worse and worse for him and he kept getting deeper and deeper in the pit. (No pun intended.) I imagine that the last few years of his imprisonment in Egypt were the hardest. Even his cell mate, the king's baker, who had promised to speak well of Joseph when he was released, forgot. Thus, a full two more years went by before a ray of hope opened up. That's a total of 13 years...a long time to wait for God's promises to come true!

I believe Joseph experienced the three emotional states of discouragement, confusion and depression. He was human, just as we; and I'm sure that the 'natural' Joseph came close to giving in to circumstances.

But, he didn't! In the narrative of Joseph's life (Genesis 37-50), we read: *"All who saw Joseph knew that God was with him."* In other words, even during his horrific time of imprisonment, Joseph didn't let himself become dismayed. He never gave up! He was able to hold on to his faith by making the correct choices—by catching and giving to God his discouragement and confusion, even when everything and everyone around him continued to betray him and let him down.

Joseph, as well as many of the great saints of Hebrews 11, "judged God faithful who had promised" even though many of them never saw how God would accomplish His promises. Nonetheless, they were persuaded that, in His way and His timing, God would miraculously perform what He had promised. And, of course, we all know how their stories ended—in victory!

All of them "staggered not at the promise of God through unbelief, but were strong in faith, giving glory to God, and being fully persuaded that, what he had promised, he was able also to perform." (Romans 4:20)

God's promises are true and will come to pass! But, it's up to Him to determine HOW and WHEN!

So, the first thing we must do when a trial or tragedy hits, is to choose by faith to trust that God knows exactly *what* He is doing and *why* He is doing it. We mustn't allow ourselves to get mired in confusion or discouragement. Remember Mark 9:24, "Lord, I believe; help Thou mine unbelief."

Why is Faith So Important?

Joseph, as well as many other Biblical saints, are perfect examples of "naked faith." No matter what they saw, felt or what their crises were, they chose by faith to obey God, trust Him and love Him. And, God made them all incredible witnesses to His faithfulness.

Such unconditional faith is important because *it affects everything we think, say and do.* It is strengthened when we choose to believe in the unfailing character, faithfulness and perfect Love of God, no matter what events surround us. Conversely, our faith is weakened when we choose to wallow in fear, doubt, confusion and depression. It's virtually impossible to separate faith from life itself, because every decision we make comes either from faith in Someone or in something.

As Paul declared in Galatians 2:20, "I am crucified with Christ: nevertheless, I live; yet not I, but Christ liveth in me; and *the life I now live in the flesh I live by the faith [or the faithfulness] of the Son of God,* who loved me and gave Himself for me."[27]

Paul is saying here that he lives Christ's life by the faith that He has in the faithfulness of God.[28] And the same should be said of us. We live Christ's life today by the faith we have in His faithfulness. Not "blindly" believing, but "wisely" trusting that He loves us and that everything He allows in our lives is for our growth. It's the conviction that He will work all things together for good because we *love* (*agapao*) Him and are surrendered to Him. (Romans 8:28) Naked faith holds Him to His promises.

Job, of course, is another example of one who lived by faith. Although Job groaned in his present circumstances, he didn't lose confidence in the future. He *never* stopped believing that God would somehow act as his Vindicator, his Advocate and his Avenger. In the midst of his greatest suffering he proclaimed,

"I know that my redeemer lives." (Job 19:25) And again, "Though He slay me, yet will I trust Him." (Job 13:15)

When the testings were over, God returned to Job twice as much as he had before. (Job 42:10)

An Example: "Living by Faith"

I can't leave the subject of "living by faith" without telling the wonderful story of George Mueller, a young man in the early 1800's who was called by God to minister to the orphans of Bristol, England. I mentioned this story in *Faith in the Night Seasons*, but it's so appropriate I want to repeat it here.

Even though Mr. Mueller had already mastered six languages and was brilliant in his own right, he never received a salary for what he did. He was supernaturally given the necessary money, through God's providence, to build three orphanages, house and feed almost 2,000 children; buy all the furniture and supplies needed to furnish and run the homes and schools; and hire all the needed personnel to manage the facilities. Extraordinary!

Mr. Mueller always expected God to answer his prayers and watched for His blessings on his labor of love. And he always received them, because *he lived by faith*.

Mr. Mueller believed that faith rested upon the Word of God. He used to say, "When sight ceases, then faith has a chance to work." As long as there was any possibility of human success, he felt faith could accomplish nothing. Thus his motto was, "God is able to do this; I cannot."

His greatest desire was to live a public life of faith so that others' trust in God would be strengthened. Mr. Mueller felt it would be living proof that faith works if he as a poor man (without asking the aid or finances of anyone), simply by prayer and faith could have all his needs met.

And, they always were! Thus, when there was no money, as happened often, he would simply say, "The Lord in His wisdom and love has not sent help, but I believe in due time He will." And He, of course, always did!

To me, Mr. Mueller epitomized Galatians 3:11, "The just shall live by faith."

Twentieth-Century Faith

We are products of the 20th century; and in this kind of "do it now" world—with fast foods, home movies and drive-through stores—many of us will struggle in this new realm of pure faith, just as a swimmer fights the powerful current that draws him into deeper water. And unless we quiet our fears and calmly rest in the Lord's hands, just like that swimmer we will drown. God uses the absence of our ability to see and understand to accomplish His will in our lives. This is the way He has chosen to work. And we must learn to trust Him in it, even if it's opposite to what we want.

When God allows painful circumstances into our lives, often we think He is punishing us or that He has somehow forsaken us. Yet *nothing* could be further from the truth. He simply wants to see our responses. Will we continue to trust and love Him when everything around us is falling apart? Will we continue to renew our minds when our worlds collapse? Will we choose, by faith, to do His will even when all we hoped for falls away?

Jesus even asks in Luke 18:8, "When the Son of man cometh, shall He find faith on earth?"

There seems to be such a spirit of heaviness over so many Christians now: broken hearts, deep sorrow, grief, self-pity, excessive mourning, rejection, buried hurts...[30] More than ever before, we must learn how to recognize these things and make the necessary choices to give them over to God and choose to have naked faith anyway.

Faith That Overcomes

The key to this kind of overcoming faith is simply choosing to *put off* anything "that is not of faith" and *to put on* Christ.[30] This, plus totally giving ourselves over to Him and having unconditional faith are the three keys of obedience that will allow us to endure to the end.

1 John 5:4 tells us that naked faith is the victory that not only overcomes the world and the flesh but, as well, the victory that overcomes the devil. Only this kind of faith can repel the enemy. Only this kind of faith can quench discouragement, confusion and depression. And only this kind of faith can lead to intimacy with the Father and the ability to endure with patience all He allows. When we lose faith, we leave ourselves wide open for the enemy's vicious **cycle of defeat**. He knows that faith and doubt cannot co-exist; therefore he does everything in his power to trap us into unbelief. He knows that unbelief will immediately destroy our sensitivity to God's voice, our ability to trust Him and our reliance upon His Word.

This is what I see happening all over in the Christian Body today. Satan is on an all-out attack in each of our lives to interject the "big three" of discouragement, confusion and depression, because he knows they will lead us to despair and defeat and the feeling of giving up. If we don't recognize <u>his</u> tactics and <u>our</u> choices, we'll never survive!

Overcoming faith requires our giving God permission to penetrate our souls with His fire of Love and to burn up <u>all</u> that is not of Him. Overcoming faith is abandoning ourselves to Him, even in the depths of our suffering. It is trusting not only what He does *through* us but also what He does *towards* us.

Conclusion

During our trials and difficulties, God leads us away from depending upon *self*—what we can see, feel and experience—to depending totally and completely upon *Him*. This is a stripping away process and the reason why it is called "naked" faith. However, just like obedience and love, this type of faith does <u>not</u> come easily or naturally. It's a learned experience. Again, it begins with one faith choice.

It's similar to the Christian sanctification process. When we first come to Christ, we really don't understand what it means to totally surrender ourselves to Him. While we are positionally saved, we haven't the slightest notion of what it means to intimately *know* Him. This deeper and more intimate love-relationship comes only as a result of total relinquishment and patient enduring.

A good test to see exactly where you are in all of this, is to ask yourself: Am I discontent in any way with what God has allowed in my life? If you are, it's an indication that you haven't fully surrendered yourself to Him. The kind of love relationship that He is after comes only as a result of complete abandonment to Him in <u>all</u> areas and <u>all</u> circumstances.

God wants to see if we really love Him. Do we really trust Him? Will we be obedient even when we can't see or understand what He is doing? Trials are one way He can find out the real answer.

Faith is *not* just a feeling: it's simply the ability to see everything that happens to us through God's eyes. As Jesus stated, "...blessed are they that have not seen, and yet have believed." (John 20:29) The Father knows that the less we "see," the more faith we'll be forced to live by.

So, in order to patiently endure our trials, we must *first* learn how to be obedient. And, the way we are obedient is by learning: 1) how to love the Lord more; 2) how to renew our minds on a daily and moment-by-moment basis; and, 3) how to develop naked faith in all circumstances.

(If you are interested in studying the subject of "worship" further, I might suggest you see our book called *Private Worship: The Key to Joy*. It shows that worship is one of the most important things a Christian can learn to do, because worship is the "key" to God's presence and His joy, His peace, His strength, His insights and His revelations. Another reason worship is so important is because Scripture tells us "we become like what we worship." If we want to become more like Jesus, we must learn to truly worship Him.)

"...he endured, as seeing Him who is invisible."
(Hebrews 11:27)

Chapter 6
"Seeing Him who is Invisible"

In the Midst of the Storm

Now, we move on to how we can see the Lord in the midst of the storm.

In my book, *Faith in the Night Seasons*, I spoke about the eagle as a *symbol* of the renewal process that God desires in each of our lives. One of the attributes of the eagle is the instinct to know exactly how long it will take before an approaching storm actually breaks. He will then fly to the highest spot he can find and wait for the winds to come. When the storm finally does come, the eagle will set his wings so that *the wind will pick him up and lift him higher above the storm*. He does not seek to escape the storm but simply uses it to lift him higher, rising on the very winds that bring the storm. Thus, while the storm rages beneath, the eagle is soaring in the sky far above with his eyes directly upon the sun. In short, **he endures in the storm by keeping his eyes upon the sun!**[31]

And this is exactly what God desires for each of us when He allows "storms" or "trials" or "tragedies" into our lives. He wants us to soar like the eagle in the midst of our storms, *patiently* enduring by keeping our eyes upon Him, seeing only Him who is invisible. Throughout it, we will enjoy a "peace that passes all understanding" even in the middle of the storm.

All of us are going to experience trials, but if we can keep our eyes directly focused upon the Son and allow these times to bring us closer to the Lord, then

*the storms will <u>not</u> have overpowered us, but actually
empowered us into the very presence of Jesus.*

Thus, it's not the trials and the tragedies of life that
weigh us down but again, how we handle them. This
is what determines *how, when* and *if* we come out of
our storm.

Review

Now that we are familiar with the first six steps or
levels of God's **cycle of trust**—knowing *His will* and
His Love which enable us to *obey Him* (by *loving Him,
renewing our minds* and *holding on to unconditional
faith)*—we can go on and discuss the seventh level,
which is how we can *see Him who is invisible* in all
things.

Only in knowing God's Love and His will, are
we able to obey Him. And only as we obey Him will
we be able to "see" Him in all things. Remember,
**His Love is what produces our obedience which
then brings about His Presence and the ability to
persevere.** It doesn't work any other way! Obedience
always precedes revelation and manifestation.
Remember Moses on the mountain. It was only *after*
he was obedient and did what God told him, that the
Lord revealed Himself. Throughout the Bible, this
principle is apparent over and over again: obedience
must precede revelation.

Speaking of Moses, Hebrews 11:27 tells us that
he *"endured [all his trials by] seeing Him who is
invisible."* In other words, he learned the fruit of
longsuffering, or endurance, by being able to see Him
in the hard times. The same is true of us.

If we don't understand the principles of obedience
that we have just learned, we won't be able to see

Him or make it through the coming rough times. Throughout this book, we have emphasized that the way we respond to our trials determines our whole spiritual walk. Whether we advance, withdraw or simply stay where we are (which is actually impossible) depends upon our moment-by-moment choices. Thus, some of us will <u>never</u> advance beyond the beginning stages of maturity to the fruit of longsuffering because rather than trust the Lord, we'll grow impatient and seek a means by which we can escape the trial, rather than stay the course. This choice is disastrous because God, in His Love, will only repeat the lesson all over again. Consequently, we must learn to cooperate fully with Him and endure, as obediently and as patiently as we can, all that He allows.

The culmination of the principles of trust is the ability to "see Him who is invisible." This means seeing all that happens to us from <u>His</u> perspective and <u>His</u> hand and <u>for our good</u>. It means having God ever before our eyes. Remember Acts 2:25, "I foresaw the Lord always before my face; for He is on my right hand, that I should not be moved." Just like that eagle, we must always keep our eyes focused upward on the Lord.

An Example: Seeing the Savior in the Midst of Everything

An incredible example of a Christian who endured his horrific trial by constantly "seeing Him who is invisible" is Richard Wurmbrand, a Romanian Pastor who spent 16 years in a Communist prison.

Pastor Wurmbrand was involved in the Christian underground movement. He met with groups of Christians in homes, basements, army barracks and woods, knowing full well what the cost of his actions would be. The Communists were determined to do whatever they could, to stamp out these Christian cells. Eventually, the pastor and his Christian brothers and sisters were exposed and captured.

Taken from his wife and son in 1948, Pastor Wurmbrand spent three years in a slave labor camp, three years in solitary confinement and five more years in a mass cell. He was released after eight years, only to be re-arrested two years later and sentenced to 25 more years. He ended up spending a total of 16 years in prison.

His wife was confined to another prison where the women were repeatedly raped, made to work at hard labor, forced to eat grass and rats and snakes and stand alone for hours at a time. At the time of their arrest, their son was only nine and was left to roam the streets of their city.

Many of the Christians who were arrested with him lost their faith, as they were brainwashed by the Communists. Some even ended up joining the party and denouncing their brothers and sisters. It was a horrifying time. The human torture was beyond anything one could ever imagine. In the words of one prisoner, "All the Biblical descriptions of hell and the pain of *Dante's Inferno* are nothing compared with the torture in the Communist prisons."

Pastor Wurmbrand had such unyielding faith that he was able to resist the brainwashing, the torture and the persecution. Someone once asked him, "How could you do that?" His simple reply was, *"Christians could be happy even there **because they saw the Savior in the midst of everything.**"*

By the late 60's, Wurmbrand and his wife were finally reunited with each other and with their son, and they began an incredible ministry called "The Voice of the Martyrs."

What Does "Seeing God" Mean?

So, what's the practical application here? How can we "see" the Lord in all things?

The Greek word for "to see" is *eido* and it comes from the root word *oida* which means "to know intimately." Remember Job. He acknowledged that after all his trials he came to know (or see) God as never before: "I have heard of Thee by the hearing of the ear [beginning knowledge of God], but now mine eye *seeth* Thee." (Now I have *intimate, experiential* knowledge of You).[32]   (Job 42:5)   Seeing God culminates, then, into an intimate, loving relationship with Him.

When we come to intimately knowing God, we will begin to "<u>see</u>" (*eido*) all that we have known so far only by "faith." Matthew 5:8 states it this way: the "pure in heart [and spirit] shall *see* God." *Purity is a prerequisite for seeing Him or knowing Him.* Only when our soul and spirit are cleansed (by the constant renewing of our mind), can God's light shine forth so that it can be said we see Him "face to face." As Hebrews 12:14 declares: "Follow peace with all men, and *holiness, without which no man shall see the Lord.*" And Matthew 5:8 teaches us "blessed are the pure in heart; for they shall *see* God."

Practical Things We Can Do To 'See Him'

Seeing the Lord not only means seeing Him in all His glory, hearing from Him and receiving from Him, but it also means giving Him permission to penetrate our souls with His fire of Love and to burn up <u>all</u> that is not of Him. It's opening ourselves up to the true depths of reality—not only believing and trusting in what He does *through us,* but also in what He does *towards us.*

Moreover, seeing God for who He is also reveals to us who we are. It exposes our true motives and our real self. As Job 42:6 tells us what happened when Job finally *saw* God, *"Wherefore I abhor myself, and repent in dust and ashes."* The very same thing happened with Isaiah. (Isaiah 6:5)

But, what are some of the more practical things we can do in order to "see" Him in the midst of our trials and tragedies? We can learn to stand still, rest and hope in His promises, stop asking "why," cease doubting and fighting Him, guard against discouragement, stop blaming others, and, finally, put on the whole Armor of God as we begin to praise and worship Him.

Let's explore each of these in a little more detail.

Stand Still

Assuming we are living God's **cycle of trust**, including all three principles of obedience, one of the first things we can do in order to see God in the midst of our crisis is to stand still.

We must stop all activity and cease striving.[33] There is a natural, instinctive rebellion in us against what is happening called "survival." Survival implores us to do whatever we can to get through the fire as quickly as we can. It's completely unnatural for us to stand still and burn! Besides, most of the time we feel that what is happening to us is *not* deserved, *not* warranted and *not* fair. Thus, we want to take matters into our own hands and try to find our "own way" out of the fire. God tells us in Isaiah 50:10-11, however, what will happen if we do this:

> "Who is among you that feareth the Lord, that obeyeth the voice of His servant, that walketh in darkness, and hath no light? Let

him trust in the Name of the Lord, and stay upon his God. *Behold, all ye that kindle [your own] fire, [and] that compass yourselves about with sparks: [and that] walk in the light of your fire, and in the sparks that ye have kindled. This shall ye have of Mine hand; ye shall lie down in sorrow."*

Here God is saying that in order to "see Him," we must *stand still and wait for Him to part the waters for us.* We must stay quiet and keep on walking in the direction in which we were going when our troubles first began. Nothing has changed in our relationship with Him except, perhaps, our *perception* of that relationship. (Hebrews 13:5) God will close the doors for us in His timing and in His way.

The more passive and peaceful we can remain in the eye of the storm, the quicker we'll advance. In summary, learning how to endure with patience is the only answer, the only solution and the only way out.

However, because we get impatient for God to "do" something, we do exactly as Isaiah 50 tells us not to. We begin to *"light our own fires."* We try to find our *own* way out—by going to more Bible Studies, by praying more, by reading the Bible more, etc. And that's when our trouble really begins. When we resist what God is trying to accomplish by *working our own way out of the trial,* we'll find ourselves in an even bigger mess. Because, the longer we prolong our trial and resist what God is doing, the sharper our suffering will become. Instead of trying to "second guess" God, we simply must wait for Him to "part the waters" for us. Consequently, we must *stand still, submit to the confusion* and *trust God anyway.*

Now, men, don't scream at me! I understand how hard this is for you "natural born fixers" to do this, especially "type A personalities" like my precious Chuck. But, this kind of *standing still* is <u>not</u> sheer passivity or inactivity on our part, *but actually is one of the most active things we can possibly do*. By an act of our will we are choosing <u>not</u> to do our "own" thing but to remain quiet and cooperate with God. This, in itself, takes an enormous amount of effort on our part. As said before, our natural inclination is to shove, fight, push, scream and yell. Standing still, *yielding our members to God,* is totally opposite of what we want to do. It seems unnatural and awkward and thus requires an active faith on our part. [34]

An Example: Beautiful Anita

A real life example of someone who *did* stand still and who *did* yield her members to God, when, humanly, I'm sure she wanted to fight, scream and yell, was a beautiful woman named Anita Brand.

Anita's story began about seven years ago when she was told that she had terminal cancer. She and her husband Paul were in their thirties at that time, and had four small children. Even though the doctors gave them a pretty discouraging prognosis, Anita and Paul decided they would look beyond the dismal medical report and put their faith in God's provisions for healing.

Paul was convinced that Anita's life belonged to the Lord, and that He would take her home *only* when He was ready. Consequently, they began a path of healing, not only using procedures that the doctors recommended but also their own homeopathic cures together with prayer, trust, obedience, surrender and relinquishment.

We all watched in utter amazement as this beautiful sister in the Lord made a miraculous recovery. From being hospitalized and completely bedridden, unable to even sit up or eat, to where she was able to accompany 250 of us to Israel the following year! She used no wheelchair, no walker and no cane. She was the first one up every morning, the first one in line for whatever sightseeing climb or adventure was planned for that day, and the first one on the bus. Everyone marveled at her tremendous faith and trust in God. What a witness she was to all of us.

Because Anita was able to stand still and wait upon the Lord, her friends said she developed a *heightened sensitivity to others*. She seemed to just know when others were in trouble, sick or afraid or hurt. She would call them up, pray for them and continue to look for ways to help them.

On Valentine's night a little over three years later, God's perfect timing came. Six hours before she closed her eyes for the last time, she sat up in bed, had dinner with all her family and friends around her, opened gifts and sang and praised God with all her heart. Later that night, Jesus came and carried her home.

Anita is a perfect example of one who accepted a situation that she could not fully understand, *stood still in it* and was no longer troubled by it. Anita lived God's **cycle of trust**. She saw God in an intimacy with Him that most of us have only read about. And, because of that, she was able patiently to endure all that the Lord allowed into her life.

In the Introduction, remember, we shared that the root of the word "longsuffering" (patient enduring) is *thumos* which means to "hold back or restrain what we really feel and want to do and, instead, do what God wants us to do." Anita demonstrated this principle perfectly.

Rest and Hope in His Promises

Another practical step we can take in order to see God in the midst of our trial is to get our eyes off the crisis, and simply <u>rest and hope in His promises</u>.

The way we lay hold of God's promises is by making choices to believe Him, no matter how we feel or what we think, knowing that He will align our feelings with those faith choices in His timing and in His way.[35] We also can claim His promises by crying out to Him;[36] by quoting Scriptures back to Him; and by listening for His answers in the Word.

Anita's friends said that she did this constantly. She had written out on 3x5 cards, every promise of healing in the entire Bible and she had them posted everywhere—in the kitchen, bathroom, car, on the floor, on chairs, on the walls. She knew these Scriptures by heart because God had engraved them there. Thus, she would pray them and quote them continually.

All we can ask is that God keep His promises to us in His timing and in His way.

Again, we mustn't move out of the Spirit to do our "own" works. Struggling or becoming agitated only makes matters worse. God has <u>not</u> changed, even though He may seem very distant at times.

We must remain pliable, implementing no self-effort on our part and waiting in peace and patience until God shows us what He wants us to do. In other words, we must endure without complaint. Remember, that's again one of the definitions of longsuffering! Jesus promises to "make the darkness light before [us]" and the "crooked things straight." (Isaiah 42:16) We must simply trust in His promise.

God will <u>not</u> lift the trial from us until He has completed <u>in us</u> the work He knows must be done. Since *He* is the One who put us in this fire to begin with, *He* must be the One to take us out.[37] There is absolutely nothing we can do to either speed up the process or to get us out of the trial faster, except to stand still, rest and hope in His promises. This, then, is just another place we must trust Him and let Him work. He will get us out of the fire in His timing and in His way.

Stop Asking Why

A further step we can take in order to "see Him who is invisible" in our trials, is to stop asking "*Why?*" This is such a big one! Remember that this is <u>not</u> a time to speak to the Lord, but a time to simply humble ourselves and know that what He is doing *in and through us* is essential for our growth.[38] He has allowed the situation and thus He is in control of it!

Consequently, it's imperative during this time to stop asking "*why?*" It's <u>not</u> a time to be vocal, but a time to accept all that He has allowed. Therefore, we must stop constantly examining ourselves and thinking, "If only I had done this or that." We must submit to the confusion and accept what is happening. Stay still, so God's Spirit can resolve it for us. *Our commission is to love God without the need to see or understand <u>what</u> He is doing or <u>why</u> He is doing it*!

Remember who God is and remember what He has done for us in the past. Remember His character. Remember that our intellect and our reason cannot help us comprehend His plans. It's only by love, endurance and patience that we can reach Him—not by our human understanding or logic. So, by faith, choose to love Him and totally give yourself over to Him, regardless of how you feel or what you think.

The important thing is <u>not</u> what God is doing, but *what God expects from us*. The only way we can overcome what our natural senses are crying out in a crisis, is by focusing all our attention on Christ. Seeing *Him who is invisible*. Eventually, our soulish life supply will be cut off, and our own natural thoughts and emotions powerless.

In the meantime, don't give way to imagination or reflection. Try to keep clearness of mind and purity of heart. Don't allow negative, self-centered or self-reflective thoughts to go unchecked to the point where you again dwell on them. Recognize these thoughts, and immediately choose to give them to God. Then, by faith, <u>do</u> as God has asked. Anything we dwell upon during this time other than God, will become an obstacle to our getting through our trial. If our mind is cluttered with other things, there will be no room for obeying, trusting and loving God.

Expect to get tired of the unrelenting struggle. Men tend to get angry. Women get emotional. It's all part of the battle. We are learning to *patiently endure all things by putting Him who is invisible in the center*. As we persevere, God will give us the necessary encouragement we need. As we actively confront our confusion and darkness through listening to the Holy Spirit's voice, searching the Word and patiently putting on our spiritual armor, He will begin to change our viewpoint amazingly and heal our lives.

Peace comes only when we accept what we cannot understand and are no longer troubled by it. The only thing we need to understand, is <u>not</u> what God is doing, but what He expects from us.

Questions That Please God

Questions we *can* ask the Lord at this time, and that are pleasing to Him are:

- Are trials normal for the Christian walk? Are they Scriptural?
- Does God really know my thoughts and my feelings? (Psalm 139:1-5)
- Is He the answer to all my needs? (Philippians 4:19)
- Is He going to help me? Does He see all that is going on? (Psalm 34:15)

These are healthy and good questions *because they are ones that the Word answers for us.* God has already given us His viewpoint on these things. Do a personal word study on them. Look up the Scriptures. Find other verses that say the same thing. Look up the Greek and Hebrew words in the Concordance.

Questions to stay away from, however, are ones that have no Scriptural answers. These are the kind of questions that can easily lead us into more doubt and confusion:

- Why is all of this happening to me? Is God angry with me?
- How could a loving Father ever do this to His child?
- What did I do to deserve it?
- Why has He forsaken me? What am I doing wrong?
- Why did He give me so much light and then turn it off?
- Why has He broken His promises to me?
- How can I ever trust Him again?
- Why has He made Himself out to be my enemy?

Entertaining these types of doubting questions will pull us down faster than anything else. We deal with these kinds of questions by taking every thought captive, recognizing them, confessing the ones that are *not of faith* and giving them to God. Remember *God loves us and everything He allows in our lives comes from that Love.* Romans 8:28 tells us that "*all* things work together for good to them that love God, to them who are the called according to His purposes."

What this is saying is that if we are totally giving ourselves over to Him, He will orchestrate everything in our life. (Psalm 86:5, 7) He delights in us and no matter what our failures and our shortcomings, He promises that He will <u>never</u> leave us or forsake us. Even if He must take us through the valley of the shadow of death in order to reproduce Himself in us, *He will never let us go.* Scripture tells us that He loves us so much that He has even engraved us on the palms of His hands. (Isaiah 49:15-16)

However, unless we begin to look at our trials through His eyes, we can easily slide into the dark abyss of doubt and unbelief, and never climb out. The purpose of this little book is to help us *see our trial* from <u>His</u> perspective and so understand the things <u>we</u> can do to patiently weather the storm. We must entrust our souls into the Father's hands, allowing the Holy Spirit to minister to and comfort us. Remember, we can only hear Him if we are clean and pure,—only if we have renewed our minds and cleansed our souls.

Cease Doubting

We have spoken about *doubt* several times before, because it's the tool Satan uses to trap us in and pull us down his **cycle of defeat**. Nevertheless, because our trials can be such a vulnerable time for us, doubt will become a major factor and thus must be highlighted.

We must not only cease striving in our own strength and ability, it's important we *cease doubting God*. As mentioned earlier, doubt brings us down faster than anything else. It devastates, paralyzes and immobilizes us simply because it affects every choice we make. Everything we think, say and do will be affected by it. Consequently, we need to recognize doubt when it first occurs, confess and repent of it and give it to the Lord—i.e., renew our minds.

Our part is to graciously *accept* our tribulations and then stand back and see what God does. If we do our part—trust and obey, He promises to do His,—reveal Himself. We must surrender ourselves to the suffering, not looking for a way out but remaining in the trial as long as God desires. Doubt immediately quenches God's involvement and closes us off to the only Source of life there is. Doubt presses us into an early spiritual death.

Therefore, if you are in the middle of a very difficult situation now and doubt has already insinuated its way into your thinking, don't wait another moment. Turn to the Lord. Go through the steps of renewing your mind, giving your doubt and unbelief over to Him. Then seek Him in the middle of your storm.

God is involved in every aspect of our existence, and there is no sorrow so great that He cannot somehow "recycle" it to bring forth blessing. Remember the example of my beautiful mom and all the Christmas and birthday gifts I received from her, even though she lay dying in a hospital.

Cease Fighting

Another area to watch out for during our trials is to <u>stop fighting God</u> and to <u>cease all efforts to deliver ourselves</u>. Instead, simply learn to lean on His breast.

Fighting God emotionally and spiritually often becomes the source of much of our trouble. We don't want to give up our sin, our self and all the things we rely upon. Yet, the more we fight to save these things, the sharper our testing will become. If we can willingly surrender ourselves to what God is doing and permit the crucifying process to go uncontested, the blows will be much softer, the process faster and the lessons quicker.

As we mentioned earlier, the battle for our lives (or the warfare against us) is waged in our minds. Thus, the less we struggle, the less it will hurt. Cease trying to figure out what God is up to and simply wait for Him to act. Cry out to Him, "Lord, I give up. I can't fight. I confess my self-pity, my rebellion. It's all yours; I'm simply going to trust You." Scripture tells us that the battle for our lives is not ours alone, but the Lord's. He has not forgotten us, and so we must stop acting as if He has. We won't be able to weather the storms like a soldier unless, we are willing to persevere. He will always be faithful.[39] Remember Romans 5:3 which tells us that *tribulation* brings about *patience*, and patience, if we allow it to, will bring about *hope*—the hope of seeing Him who is invisible.

It is God who holds us fast to the cross and it's God who will loose us from that cross when He sees fit. Nothing can change His plans. We must simply seek His strength to endure and persevere with courage, humility and love.

So, keep your eyes upon Him just like the eagle who weathers the storm by flying above it, his eyes fixed only upon the sun. Even if we don't see Him or feel Him or understand His ways in a crisis, God still promises that in His perfect timing the confusion and the darkness will eventually shrivel away and the light will begin to shine. In Psalm 112:4 the assurance is given us that for the righteous "there ariseth light in the darkness."

Guard Against Discouragement

We have touched upon discouragement before but, again, in a crisis it's imperative that we watch out for it. Disappointed hope is one of the biggest issues in the Christian body today, because, as we saw last chapter, it leads down the enemy's cycle to confusion, depression, loss of vision, disorientation, despair and defeat. Discouragement is one of the places where all these things begin! So, watch out! Deal with the first hints of it. Confess it, repent of it and then give it to God.

Notice in Psalm 38 that even the godly and righteous King David battled discouragement. Listen to his words:

"I am troubled; I am bowed down greatly; I go mourning all the day long...I am feeble and sore broken: I have roared by reason of the disquietness of my heart...My heart panteth, my strength faileth me: as for the light of mine eyes, it also is gone from me...I, as a deaf man, heard not; and I was as a dumb man that openeth not his mouth. Thus I was as a man that heareth not, and in whose mouth are no reproofs." (Verses 6, 8, 10, 13-14)

If we are honest with ourselves, we'd have to admit that much of the Christian body today suffers from depression. Why? *Because many of us have become discouraged with what God has allowed in our lives and we have not dealt with it.* (Now, there is a clinical depression that comes from a chemical imbalance in our system. This is not what I am talking about here.) The kind of depression that I believe so many Christians are struggling with today is really spiritual in nature. *It's simply unchecked disappointment at the circumstances the Lord has allowed.*

One of the definitions I found for *longsuffering* was "an attitude that's just the opposite of depression and despondency." Thus, longsuffering is always associated with a future hope. On the other hand, discouragement is one step away from hopelessness! When we become discouraged, we cling to our anxieties, fears and self-pity. This choice not only strengthens our hopelessness, it also impedes what God wants to do.

We must also be careful not to fall into the mode of wanting sympathy from others at this time. Because be assured, we won't get it! Discouragement and depression repel others. And, these things only deepen the pit that we're trying so desperately to get out of. Our eyes cannot be on anyone or anything but God Himself. It's <u>His</u> approval and <u>His</u> support that we need most, not others' pity.

The greatest failure we can make during our trials is allowing discouragement to become exaggerated. If we let these negative thoughts go unchecked, depression will most likely result, quench God's Spirit and deprive us of hearing His voice and seeing His face just when we need Him the most.

Debbie, my beloved friend and co-laborer in the ministry, confided that when discouragement creeps in on her, it's usually because she has <u>not</u> been obedient to what the Lord has previously told her to do. Again, obedience must come *before* we are able to see Him.

Stop Blaming Others

Another important thing we must do in order to "see" the Lord in the midst of our trials, is to <u>stop blaming others</u>. *When God has appointed us to suffer, He permits even the most virtuous people to be blinded towards us.* Thus, it's important *not* to harbor any resentment or bitterness against those involved in our trials. By blaming them and not forgiving them, we only condemn ourselves—which, of course, breeds more bitterness in us. We mustn't be governed by our self-righteousness or our justified feelings, but only by God's Love and wisdom. He will teach us how to "love wisely."

God will repay those truly responsible for our troubles in His timing and in His way.[40]   Scripture tells us that <u>He</u> is our defender.[41]   Psalm 94:22 tells us, "The Lord is my defense; and my God is the rock of my refuge." Only He knows the real truth and only He knows how to weave our lives together perfectly. We must neither try to vindicate ourselves, nor try to help God along. He promises to fight our battles for us.[42] We must simply stand still and wait for Him to act. (Psalm 37:3-4)

It's also important that we pray for others involved: not blame them, but simply leave them in God's care and in His hands.[43]   Thank the Lord in advance for delivering us out of *their* hands.

Furthermore, we mustn't speak about our problems to others because it only deepens our bitterness, programs those negative thoughts in deeper, and gives the enemy another entrance in us. Try to speak well of others involved. Ephesians 4:29 tells us, "Let no corrupt communication proceed out of your mouth, but that which is good to the use of edifying, that it may minister grace unto the hearers." Of course God will give us certain confidants whom we <u>can</u> trust and share the truth with. But we must be careful not to confide with everyone for, be assured, such will come back to haunt us.

I know how very difficult a discipline this is, especially when by the world's standards we are "justified" for being angry and bitter. But sharing our negative feelings and emotions about others at this time only makes *us* more miserable, the enemy happier and the whole process prolonged. I know! I've been there!

As well, when something bad happens, we mustn't run first thing to a friend or to the phone, but choose instead to go to be alone with the Lord. Reaffirm to Him that all that matters to you is obeying, loving and seeing Him. Quote Psalm 73:25 to Him, "*Whom have I...but Thee?*" Choose, by faith, to say as Job did, "For I know that my redeemer liveth and...in my flesh, shall I see God." (Job 19:26)

"Fast" from expecting any emotional or intellectual security in knowing, understanding and being right. Be patient, believe in God and listen for His voice. He knows your every thought and experience and is aware of what you want and what you need. Trust Him implicitly.

Finally, submit to the confusion. Even you guys! *Put all your reason, as well as your emotions, aside and look only to God. Our human reason cannot cope with the situation that God has allowed. Live by faith and wait for God's Spirit to resolve the issues for you. Remain receptive, not expecting to understand all of God's ways but simply trusting Him in them. This, again, is the appropriate time to say and mean, by faith, "Though You slay me, yet will I trust You..."*

Put On The Armor of God

Another vital thing we must do in order to "see Him" while we patiently endure our trials, is <u>to put on the whole Armor of God</u>! The older I become in the Lord, the more I realize the absolute necessity of doing this.

> Ephesians 6:10 tells us: "Finally, my brethren, *be strong* in the Lord, and in the power of *His* might."

Our most crucial imperative at this time—not a suggestion, but a command—is to "be strong in the Lord." The word *strong* here is in the present tense which implies *continuous*. It's also in the passive voice, which means <u>we</u> are the ones who receive the action. In other words, it's something that remains established within us. [44]

As we consider the warfare we are engaged in, remember that "we wrestle not against flesh and blood, but against principalities, against powers, against the rulers of the darkness of this world, against spiritual wickedness in high places." (Ephesians 6:12)

Paul details the seven elements of the Armor of God that we must have on daily (Ephesians 6:14-18):

1) "having your loins girded about with truth" (Jesus is the Truth)

2) "having on the breastplate of righteousness" (His Righteousness)

3) "your feet shod with the preparation of the gospel of peace" (Putting off our sin and putting on Christ)

4) "Above all, taking the shield of faith, with which ye shall be able to quench all the fiery darts of the wicked" (Faith choices to trust and obey God unconditionally)

5) "take the helmet of salvation" (Our security in Christ)

6) "and the sword of the Spirit, which is the Word of God" (Exposing Satan's lies)

7) "praying always with all prayer and supplication in the Spirit" (Our heavy artillery)

Go through these steps daily. Be sure you have each item "put on" securely. If you do your part, God will surely do His. And, you will never be caught off guard!

Praise God

Moreover, in order to "see Him who is invisible" during our trials, we must learn to praise God. Many of us have quoted 1 Thessalonians 5:18: "In everything give thanks; for this is the will of God in Christ Jesus concerning you."[45] Even so, by faith, we need to begin to walk out this Scripture. (Philippians 4:4, 6-7)

Praise can be seen as the "glue" that keeps us looking "up" during our trials. Scripture tells us that "God inhabits [our] praises." (Psalm 22:3) Praise is the action that keeps our eyes focused on the Lord, not on our circumstances. Praise is what changes our complaints into compliments!

We must thank the Lord, by faith, for all that He is doing in our lives, for all that He has done in the past and for what He is going to do in the future.[46] We are praising and thanking Him <u>not</u> for the trial, but for *who He is* during the trial—our strength, our redeemer, our shepherd guide. By praising Him, Scripture says that we will pierce the darkness and the evil spirits will flee away. The enemy hates the Name of Jesus and he despises the praises of God. (So, try praising God and watch the enemy flee.)

Prayers like: "Jesus, You are my King, my Lord...I seek only You, my Love, my Life..." Tell Him over and over again how much you love Him. Let the Holy Spirit remind you of all the Names of God and all the words you can think of about His character. He wants us to thank Him and praise Him for His goodness, His faithfulness, His righteousness, His power, His sovereignty, His Love, His mercy, His grace, His peace, His truth, His wisdom, His redemption, His Spirit, His strength, His salvation, His sanctification and all the other numberless things that we can think of. Praising Him for these things will turn our mind from the depths of despair to being fully focused upon Him.

During a trial years ago, I remember reading the book *Prison to Praise* by Merlin Carothers and thinking, "How on earth can I praise God for all the bad things that are happening in my life?" I have since learned that what God wants us to praise Him for is <u>not</u> all the bad things, *but for who He is* in the *middle* of the bad things and for *what He is going to do in us and through us* because of the bad things.

This is the kind of praise that will get us through our trials. King David tells us, in Psalm 119:164, that He praised God seven times a day in order to "see Him who is invisible." Try it!

Remember the example of Anita Brand early in this chapter. Her family told me that she had praise music going continually in her home, in her car and that she always carried a walkman tape recorder. The last year of her life, she joined a group of believers who had a "praise night" once a month, called *Joy Jam*. Many came who were in similar circumstances as Anita. But, when they began to praise the Lord, universally their focus was turned from their illness and hardship to the Lord, and they rejoiced. Seeing Him who is invisible. God *does* inhabit our praises.

Worship the Lord

It's also imperative at this time to learn to truly worship the Lord. Worshipping the Lord is very different from simply praising Him. Praise is what opens the door to God's dwelling place, but *worship is what leads us directly into His presence*. Praise can be soulish (i.e., it <u>can</u> be done when we are in the flesh), whereas, true worship *can only* be spiritual (only be done when we are clean before the Lord and in the spirit).

Listen to Psalm 24:3-4: "Who shall ascend into the hill of the Lord? Or who shall stand in His Holy Place? He who has *clean hands*, and *a pure heart*, who hath not lifted up his soul unto vanity, nor sworn deceitfully." In other words, we cannot worship God when we are "in the flesh," but only when we are cleansed and in "the beauty of His holiness." Consequently, the only person who can enter God's presence, see and worship Him, is one who has set his sin and self aside and is truly in the spirit.

The reason worship is so critical at this time is because worship not only leads us to the presence of the Lord, but also to His joy. Psalm 16:11 tell us that in the presence of the Lord there is "fulness of joy." The reason so many of us are joyless, especially in our trials, is because we're not true worshippers. John 4:23-24 tells us that, "the true worshippers shall worship the Father in spirit and in truth." Thus, true worship can lead us to being joyful *no matter what our circumstances are.* Worship not only brings us joy, it also gives us the strength of the Lord. Remember Nehemiah 8:10: "the joy of the Lord is your strength." The strength of the Lord is what will get us through the hard times. So, learning to worship the Lord during our trials is vital. (If you want to learn more about worship and joy and its practical application, pick up our new book, *Private Worship: The Key to Joy*.)

Do Spiritual Warfare

Last, but certainly not least, in order to see the Lord more clearly in our trials, we must learn how to do spiritual warfare. We learned a few minutes ago how to put our armor on, now we must learn how to use it.

Spiritual warfare must go along side of worship (and putting on the Armor of God) because when we begin to worship the Lord on a daily basis, we'll encounter the enemy more than we ever have before. The enemy is determined to derail worshippers in any way he can. So, worshipping the Lord and fighting the enemy go hand in hand. We cannot do one without the other. Therefore, a part of our prayer time in the Holy Place must be concerned with binding the enemy, loosing his strongholds and commanding him to leave in the Name and Power of Jesus Christ.

If you are like me, when you pray, especially with a new prayer, it's always helpful to have a rough example to follow. Yes, it's true the Holy Spirit must always *lead* our prayers, but it's also useful to have a guideline when you are just beginning. So here is an idea of how you might begin to pray against the enemy. (If this prayer doesn't meet your needs, then, by all means, let the Holy Spirit write your own.)

Abba Father, King of the Universe, in the Name of Jesus, I ask you to search out and expose all my enemies and the tactics they employ against me. Open my eyes that I may see and understand the battle. Give me wisdom and understanding that I may lean on Your ways and not my own.

Reveal any root of bitterness, unforgiveness or iniquity that I may repent before you and take back any legal right given to the enemy. Bind the enemy that is round about me and loose every stronghold that has been established in my life. In the name of Jesus and through His authority I say to my enemies, "the Lord rebuke you for He is my defender and the lifter of my soul. I take my stand against you, your temptations, deceptions and snares in the Name of the Lord Jesus Christ."

Father, Creator of all things, let me not take my stand alone, but fill me with Your Spirit. Empower me to stand against the enemy and cover me with the blood of Jesus. Release Your mighty angels to defend. I trust in You, Jehovah-Jireh, my provider, and I will not be disappointed, for you are a shield about me. Amen.

Conclusion

In conclusion, it's not that all our trials and tribulations will go away when we do the before-mentioned practical things, but by doing these things, we'll learn how to "see" (just a little bit clearer) the Lord in the midst of them. And because we can see Him we'll have the ability to patiently endure, a little more effectively, all that He has allowed. Then, we can claim all the Scriptural promises we learned in Chapter One.

- Mark 13:13, "...he that shall <u>endure</u> unto the end, the same *shall be saved.*"

- 2 Timothy 2:10, "...[those] that <u>endure</u> all things...*may also obtain the salvation* which is in Christ Jesus with eternal glory."

- Hebrews 12:7, "If ye <u>endure</u> chastening, God dealeth with you as with *sons...*"

- Revelation 3:10, "Because [you] have kept the word of My <u>patience,</u> I also will *keep [you] from the hour of temptation,* which shall come upon all the world to try them."

- James 5:11, "Behold, we count them *happy* who <u>endure.</u>"

- 1 Corinthians 13:4 & 7, "*Love*...beareth all things, believeth all things, hopeth all things, *<u>endureth</u> all things.*"

- And finally, James 1:12, "Blessed is the man that <u>endureth</u> temptation; for when he is tried, he shall receive the *crown of life.*"

Consequently, rather than feeling "lost" during our difficult crisis, we'll actually be able to "find" ourselves. We'll know that the Lord is simply clearing away the debris in our lives, so that He can conform us more into His image. We'll also be convinced that He is pouring forth *through us* <u>all</u> the fruit of the Spirit— not only His Love, peace and joy but also His fruit of longsuffering, patient enduring and perseverance.

Again, the question is: "Will we allow Him to do all that He needs to in order to bring about these things?

"My brethren, count it all joy when ye fall into various trials, knowing that the testing of your faith produces patience. But let patience have its perfect work, that you may be perfect and complete, lacking nothing." (James 1:2-4)

Chapter 7
Patiently Enduring All Things

So, obedience comes <u>before</u> sight—before we are able to "see Him who is invisible." Remember God's **cycle of trust**: *Knowing His will and His Love produces our obedience which brings about His presence and the ability to patiently endure all things.*

Our goal as Christians should not simply be the security of our salvation, but the ability to see God face to face, just as Moses did. Exodus 34:29-30 describes Moses as so touched and so changed by his encounter with the Lord, that his face shone. His face actually radiated on the outside what had occurred to him on the inside. And that same thing can happen to us. Obviously, not to the degree that it happened with Moses, but all of us, at one time or another, have met those special people whose countenance just glows because they have been with Jesus. They have been in His presence, and it shows.

In this wonderful state of experiencing God's presence, we'll begin to watch Him repay our painful times with His unfathomable Love and affection. We'll also begin to understand that in our dark seasons, He <u>never</u> really left us at all. He just had to move, in order to bring us to this point of intimacy.[47] "And ye shall know that I have not done *without cause* all that I have done...saith the Lord." (Ezekiel 14:23)

This truth alone should render us *incapable of doubting* and give us the assurance that He's *always* known what He was doing.[48]

How fortunate we are if in a trial we can, at least, understand God's overall plan: that He has not forsaken us, that He has not left us and that we have not misunderstood Him, but that He is simply using our trials, our tribulations and our tragedies to conform us more into His image. How blessed we are if we know that He is simply drawing us into the realm of pure faith. A realm where we won't have to rely on our feelings, our understanding or what we see, but one where we'll have <u>no</u> other choice but to depend totally upon Him. If we can make it to this state of mind, then we'll be able to submit with patience and endurance to the confusion in our life, and by faith accept it. We'll be able to trust the Holy Spirit to resolve the problems for us and to love God *without the need to see or understand exactly what He is doing.*

I know how difficult this is to do. In our natural state, when we are hurting and fearful and confused, it's almost impossible to trust Him unconditionally without the understanding of what's going on. But this is the very moment that it's critical to choose to say "Though You slay me, yet will I trust You." (Job 13:15)

How we behave during our time of affliction will exemplify to others, not only the fruit of love, peace and joy, but also the fruit of longsuffering. If we can learn patience in enduring our trials through obeying and unconditionally trusting Him, we'll be able to reflect that intimacy to others.

The following are some incredible examples of patient enduring that we can model in our own behavior:

Abraham

In Genesis 15, Abram receives a divine word from the Lord. The Lord tells him he shall have a son of his own. (Verse 4) Abram believed God and it was counted to him for righteousness. Later, however, Abram goes back and questions the Lord as to how he will know that he will inherit the promise. (Verse 8) Whereupon, the Lord again confirms His promise to him with an elaborate covenant. (Verse 9-10) Shortly after this, Abram experiences a horrifying dark night of terror. In Scripture it's called "a horror of great darkness." (Verse 12) After which there is silence from heaven on this subject for 13 years! So instead of the blessing that Abram expected, no answer comes at all. Thirteen years is a *long* time to wait for a personal promise to be answered!

But at the end of the 13 years, the Lord again appears to Abram. Now, He renews His covenant with him, changes his name to Abraham and again promises him a son. The Lord makes the same promise to Sarai, changing her name to Sarah. (Genesis 17) Sarah laughs at the prospect of having a baby at 100 years old, but God responds, "Is anything too hard for the Lord?" (Genesis 18:14)

We must remember this also! In our most difficult circumstances, we must focus on the fact that God can do *all* things, nothing is too tough or formidable for Him!

In Genesis 21, all of God's promises are fulfilled. The Lord does unto Sarah just as He promised and even "at the exact set time" He had promised. At this point it had been 14 years since Abraham received his first promise! Sarah called the baby Isaac (which means, "all will laugh when they hear about this"). Note that God was faithful to His promise and carried out His purposes exactly as foretold, even though, to Sarah and Abraham, God's Word seemed utterly impossible!

Then, God again tests Abraham by asking that he sacrifice Isaac, the son for whom he had waited so long. (Genesis 22) Abraham by faith immediately obeys, even though he must have personally struggled tremendously. But just as Abraham is to kill Isaac, the Lord stops him and says, "*Now* I know that you fear Me, seeing that you did not withhold Isaac from Me." The Lord then tells Abraham that He intends to bless him abundantly and multiply his seed "as the stars of the heavens."

Note the fascinating progression of events here:

1) First, there is the original promise.
2) Then, there's the questioning.
3) Then, there's the "dark night."
4) Then, there's a 13-year silence where Abraham learns patient endurance.
5) Then, there's a reconfirmation of the promise
6) Then, the promise is fulfilled.
7) Then, the Lord asks for the promise to be sacrificed.
8) Finally, after Abraham's obedience and longsuffering, the Lord promises more blessings.

I find this pattern extremely interesting, because God has worked in my own life in a very similar way. Do you see any parallels in your life?

Also, contrast Romans 5:3-5 here: first, *tribulation*; then, *patience*; then, *experience*; then, *hope*; and finally, *love*.

Joseph

Another example of one who saw God in the midst of his devastating trial and responded as God would have him, is of course, Joseph. If anyone was justified in being angry, asking why, doubting God, fighting the circumstances, blaming others, being discouraged and dismayed, Joseph certainly was!

You remember the story: God gave Joseph an incredible dream that contained great personal promises for the future. Joseph made the mistake, however, of telling his brothers about his dream, and it left them seething with jealousy. They hated him for it. They tied him up, threw him into a pit, and ended up selling him to a caravan of Ishmaelites on their way to Egypt. Joseph eventually was bought by Potiphar, a high-ranking Egyptian official, whose wife repeatedly tried to seduce the devout young Hebrew. When she found that she could not, she accused the innocent Joseph of trying to molest her. As a result, Potiphar angrily threw the young man into prison, where he remained for years. When Joseph was finally released from prison, as a result of divinely-orchestrated circumstances, he had patiently endured for a total of *13 years!*

Again, 13 years! Interesting? Just a coincidence? I wonder.

The Bible tells us that Joseph unconditionally forgave his brothers even *before* they ever came to ask his forgiveness. Clearly, he didn't hold on to his "justified" feelings of unforgiveness, bitterness and resentment, but continually gave them over to the Lord. He said to his brothers, "But as for you, you thought evil against me; but God meant it unto good." (Genesis 50:20) In spite of his horrific trial, Joseph stayed open and clean before the Lord. And, as we saw last chapter, Scripture tells us that all who saw Joseph knew that "*God was with Him.*" He was able to patiently endure because he unconditionally obeyed God. He saw Him "who is invisible" in his circumstances. And, he reflected that relationship in all that he did.

God never left Joseph. He never abandoned him. He remained with him and worked through him the whole time. Joseph understood God's will for his life and thus, he had enough faith to allow God to manifest Himself through him, even in his darkest night.

The very end of Joseph's story is that the Lord placed him as the supreme leader over all of Egypt, with his brothers in his service. The Lord, who had always been his defense and avenger, worked out His perfect will through him.

Again, notice that the progression of events in Joseph's story are very similar to those of Abraham:

1) First, the original promise
2) Then, the questions
3) Then, the dark night
4) Then, the 13-year silence (where Joseph learned longsuffering)
5) Then, the reconfirming of the promise
6) And, finally, the promise fulfilled

What's missing is the testing of the fulfilment of the promise.

The amazing thing about this story of Joseph is that, regardless of what was going on in his life, the Scripture says that all who saw him "knew God was with him." In other words, he *always reflected the Lord*. This, of course, is God's will for each of us. No matter what is going on, we are still to show forth God's Love and His life. The only way this is possible is by obedience and trust, thus seeing Him who is invisible in all things.

God not only creates the brightness of day, He also creates the darkness of night.[49] He not only is the Author of our joy and gladness, He is also the Author of our night seasons. Too many Christians have chosen to recreate God in their own image. They tell themselves that since no loving father would ever allow his children to suffer hardship, neither would a heavenly Father! If we put God into a box built by our own human understanding, we'll never be able to endure the trials of our faith. Joseph survived those long 13 years by his unwavering faith in the goodness and faithfulness of God. So must we!

What can we learn from Joseph's story? First, we can emulate how he handled his brothers. He unconditionally forgave them, even before they came and asked him for it. We must do the same. We must not only forgive others, we must also pray for them, leave them in God's hands and not blame them. Only God knows the real truth and only He knows how to fight our battles for us. Scripture tells us that the Lord will repay those truly responsible for our troubles in His timing and in His way.[50] And we've seen this to be true in the before-mentioned stories. As Psalm 94:22 promises, "The Lord is [our] defense" and our avenger. Thus, we must neither try to vindicate ourselves, nor help the Lord along by lighting our own fires. We must simply stand still, forgive them, pray for them and then, watch God work.

Like Joseph, we can learn how to reflect Christ in all circumstances—in all our trials—as we learn to love God more, renew our minds and hold on to unshakeable faith. Then all who come into contact with us, even in our dark times, will say, "Truly, God is with them,"—just as they did Joseph.

If we only believe in a God of easy comfort, how can our faith ever withstand the heat of harsh circumstances? Like grass without roots that go deep into the soil, we will surely wither and die. Our faith must unconditionally be rooted in God's Love and His faithfulness in order to withstand the difficult

circumstances that might come along.   God is in
control and He knows exactly what He is doing.

A Modern Day Joseph: Diana

A modern day example of trusting the Lord
unconditionally and, like Joseph, patiently enduring
all things, was my dear friend Diana Bandtlow. I have
spoken about Diana in many of my books. But I know
of no greater example.

Diana was only 27 years old and just two years
a Christian, when she was diagnosed with leukemia
and given only six months to live. She had a beloved
husband, Ed, who adored her, and two precious
children, Hillary, then 3 and Stephanie, 1.

Diana had tremendous faith in God, the kind of
faith we all aspire to. She knew that because God loved
her, He would not allow anything into her life that
wasn't "Father-filtered" and that wouldn't eventually
bring Him glory. So, throughout her ordeal, no matter
what the circumstances were and no matter how much
pain she was in, she continually chose to make "faith"
choices to trust her God and to abandon herself to His
will. She endured her predicament because she "saw
Him who was invisible."

Now you know that she must have experienced
things like fear, doubt and anger because she was
human and she was scared. But because she trusted
the Lord unequivocally and she kept making those
"contrary choices" to do His will, she was able to
reflect Him in all circumstances, just like Joseph.

Even though Diana had enough faith to "move
mountains," and had been prayed for many times by
the elders of her church, God in His sovereignty, chose
not to heal her physically. He must have known that the

example of her faith and the witness of His life through her frail condition would affect more lives than any other path He might choose. And, it's absolutely true. As I have shared Diana's story at different seminars over the last 20-25 years, many people have come up to me and told me how her life has touched them.

In particular, two nurses from California came up after one seminar and shared how they had attended Diana in the hospital the last few weeks of her life. They told that they had both come to know Jesus Christ as their Lord and Savior as a result of seeing *Christ's life* through Diana, even in her dying.

They recounted how when they would go into her room to administer her pain medication, Diana would softly whisper, "No, thank you, my Father is taking care of me." Then she would say, "And may He bless you abundantly in all you do today." Both nurses shared how totally uncharacteristic this is of terminally ill patients. They said they saw in Diana a Love, a peace and a joy that "passed all human understanding." They both yearned to have what Diana had. And so it was that, as a direct result of Diana's witness, both accepted Christ.

I know of hundreds more people affected, even to this day, by Diana's story. It proves to us that *pure faith is simply accepting a situation that we cannot fully understand and no longer being troubled by it*. Because of Diana's reactions, God was able to accomplish all that He desired in her life. And, He touched hundreds of people through her.

As it came closer to Christmas, Diana told everyone that God was going to allow her to go "home" for the holidays. Now she thought the Lord meant her earthly home, but on Christmas day, 1974, God took His precious child "home" to that one that He had prepared for her from the beginning of time. (John 14:2)

Because of Diana's incredible faith and the fruit of longsuffering in her life, I will never be the same.

One Last Example: German Pastor

One last example of a person who patiently endured his trial through obedience and "seeing Him who is invisible" is a German pastor who lived in the mid-1930's. This pastor was abducted from his church by the Nazi party because he was suspected of aiding and abetting Jews. He was immediately thrown into prison and put in a five-foot cell. There was no hearing, no trial—not even time to let his family know what had happened to him.

For weeks, this gentle pastor asked the prison guard outside his cell door if he could use the phone at the end of the hall to call his wife and family and, at least, let them know he was alive. The guard, however, was a horrible man who hated anyone and everyone who had to do with Jewry. He not only would not let the pastor use the phone, he also determined to make the pastor's life as miserable as possible.

This guard sadistically skipped the pastor's cell when meals were handed out; he made the pastor go weeks without a shower; he kept lights burning so he couldn't sleep at night; he blasted his shortwave radio, hoping the constant noise would break the pastor's will; he used filthy language; he pushed him; he shoved him; and, when he could, he arranged for him to have the most difficult job in the labor force.

The pastor, on the other hand, prayed over and over again that he not let his natural hate for this guard consume him. He prayed instead to be able to forgive him and, somehow, show him God's Love. As the months went by, whenever possible, the pastor smiled at the guard; he thanked him when his meals *did* come; when the guard was near his cell, the pastor told him about his own wife and his children; he even questioned the guard about his family and about his goals, ideas and visions; and, one time, for a quick moment, he had a chance to tell the guard about Christ and His Love.

The guard <u>never</u> answered a word, but undoubtedly he heard it all.

After months of unconditionally giving himself over to this terrible guard, God's real Love finally broke through. One night, as the pastor was again quietly talking to him, the guard cracked a smile; the next day, instead of his cell being skipped for lunch, the pastor got two meals; the following evening he was allowed not only to go to the showers, but also to stay as long as he wanted; the lights began going off at night in his cell, and the radio noise ceased. Finally, one afternoon the guard came into the pastor's cell, asked him for his home phone number, and he, personally, made the long awaited call to the pastor's family.

A few months later the pastor was mysteriously released, with no questions asked.

Supernatural Responses

The pastor's story is a perfect example of how the Lord wants each of us to react in our trials, our tribulations and tragedies. What happened in the above story was supernatural. Naturally the pastor hated his persecutor and by worldly standards was certainly justified in doing so. But he loved Jesus more than he loved himself, and he knew how God would have him to respond. Thus, he constantly made the choice to obey God by remaining still, repressing doubt, resisting discouragement, surrendering himself to the situation and trusting God anyway. And because of the pastor's godly response, that guard is now part of God's kingdom!

Like Abraham, Joseph, Diana and this precious pastor, our faith is developed over the years by the various trials and testings that God allows into our lives. James 1:3 assures us that when our faith is tested, our endurance has a chance to grow. (*Read that "longsuffering."*) What James is saying is that when our faith is tested, we have an opportunity to learn the fruit of longsuffering. *And, as a result, we can become "perfect, entire and wanting nothing."* Thus, we should rejoice when we encounter trials and problems, because these help us learn longsuffering. And *longsuffering*, remember, leads to *experience* and, then, *hope* and *love*. (Romans 5:5)

Here, again, that same progression is seen, as in Abraham's and Joseph's life. Tribulation worketh patience; patience, experience; experience, hope; hope maketh not ashamed because the Love of God is shed in our hearts. So, note that hope always comes *after* patient enduring and experience, and not before!

All these stories clearly illustrate the fact that we must *never* doubt God. We must never ask Him why, we must never fight Him or be discouraged at what He allows. *God is involved in every aspect of our existence and there is no sorrow so great that He cannot somehow "recycle" it to bring forth blessing.*

The Fellowship of His Sufferings

The discipline of barring ourselves from following what we think, feel and desire is the way God has chosen to bring redemption to a fallen world. Jesus suffered for us and gave us His example to follow. We cannot die to ourselves without suffering. The two go hand in hand. Suffering, consequently, *can be* a blessing in disguise, for it has as its goal the sanctification and purification of our souls. It comes about as God unyieldingly identifies the most potentially damaging hindrance to our relationship with Him, and then lovingly begins to strip it away. He crushes us, breaks us, shakes us and then removes that hindrance from us. Much of the time we not only don't understand *why* God has called us to suffer but that He *has* called us to suffer. C.S. Lewis once said, "The question is not why the righteous suffer, *but why some do not!"*

The Bible tells us that it's only through death that there can be life! Therefore, unless we are willing to participate in the fellowship of Christ's sufferings, we will not be equipped to participate in His exaltation (His life). Remember 2 Timothy 2:11-12, "For if we died with Him, we shall also live with Him; *if we suffer, we shall also reign with Him.*"

Alan Redpath, the notable English writer, assures us that God has brought us to this experience simply because "*He wants to [simply] replace us with Himself.*"[51] I love that! God uses our trials to simply "replace us with Himself." This is the whole Christian life in a nutshell! This is God's will: to empty us of *ourselves* so He can fill us with *Himself.* Thus, when we willingly lay our lives down to Him, He will do whatever is necessary to accomplish that will. However, if we are unwilling to allow Him to rearrange our lives, then He takes matters into His own hands. His way of turning us around and gently encouraging us to do His will, is to *allow* trials and difficulties and adversities.

Philippians 3:10 confirms that this is what "the fellowship of His sufferings" is all about. It's God's way of making us "conformable to His death." This Scripture only becomes a reality in our lives when we not only proclaim what Christ did for us on the Cross, but also when we daily experience "barring our self from sin and self" and doing His will anyway.

And, *sometimes struggles are exactly what we need in our life in order to make us all that God desires.* If God allowed us to go through life without obstacles, it would probably cripple us.

The Moth Story

There's an analogy of this that I related in the *Faith in the Night Season* book that seems very appropriate here. It's called *The Moth and the Cocoon:*[52]

"A man found a cocoon of an emperor moth. He took it home so that he could watch the moth come out of the cocoon. On the day a small opening appeared, he sat and watched the moth for several hours as the moth struggled to force its body through that little hole.

"Then, it seemed to stop making any progress. It appeared as if it had gotten as far as it could and it could go no farther. It just seemed to be stuck. The man, in his kindness, decided to help the moth. So he took a pair of scissors and snipped off the remaining bit of the cocoon. The moth then emerged easily. But, it had a swollen body and small, shriveled wings.

"The man continued to watch the moth because he expected that, at any moment, the wings would enlarge and expand to be able to support the body, which would then contract. Neither happened! In fact, the little moth spent the rest of its life crawling around with a swollen body and shriveled wings. It <u>never</u> was able to fly.

"What the man in his kindness and haste did not understand was that the restricting cocoon, and the struggle required for the moth to get through the tiny opening, were God's way of forcing fluid from the body of the moth into its wings so that it would be ready for flight once it achieved its freedom from the cocoon. Freedom and flight would come only after the struggle. By depriving the moth of this struggle, he deprived the moth of health."

Consequently, when God allows painful circumstances into our lives, we mustn't assume that He is punishing us or that He has forsaken us, because nothing could be further from the truth. God is simply attempting to free us from our soulish limitations and lead us into the wider realm of His Spirit.[53] God is drawing us into the realm of pure faith where we'll learn experientially that we <u>cannot</u> depend upon our feelings, what we see or what we think. He is bringing us to a place where we'll have no other choice but total dependence upon Him, just like the moth.

Thus, it's only through faith and longsuffering that we *can* inherit God's promises. Again, James 1:2-3 tells us, "My brethren, count it all joy when ye fall into various trials, knowing this, that the testing of your faith worketh patience. But let patience have her perfect work, *that ye may be perfect and entire, lacking nothing*." And, 1 Peter 4:12-13, "Beloved, think it not strange concerning the fiery trial which is to test you, as though some strange thing happened unto you, but rejoice, inasmuch as ye are *partakers of Christ's suffering*, that when His glory shall be revealed, ye may be glad with exceeding joy."

God's purpose for us as Christians is to mold us more and more into His image—His total image—so that we can experience not only *abundant life*, but also *intimacy with Him* (seeing Him who is invisible). Consequently, every circumstance, every situation and every experience that He allows into our lives is "God-designed" to develop these two things. If we understand what God is doing and how He wants us to act, then we can remain peaceful in our trials and patiently endure them. If, however, we don't understand what His will is or how we are to respond, then we'll end up doing everything wrong and only prolong our suffering.

Choices We Make by Faith

Christians often ask me: "How could Diana have responded as obediently as she did, when she obviously wanted to live, be a wife and see her children grow up? And, how could Joseph have responded to his brothers as he did, when he really probably wanted to kill them? Finally, how could that German pastor react so lovingly, when he truly despised that guard?"

How could all of these people have endured so patiently when, in the natural, they must have felt just the opposite?

Great question!

The answer is, they did so by making "faith choices." Faith choices or "contrary choices" are those that are *contrary to what we feel, think and desire*. But they are the only response, as we have said, that frees us from ourselves and unleashes all of God's Power to come to our aid. *To me, this is one of the most incredible gifts of all. We don't have to "feel" our choices, we simply must be willing to make them. God, then, in His perfect timing and way, does the rest.*

This means that as Christians, we can be totally honest with God and admit when we don't love someone, when we are really scared or when we don't want to forgive. But then, by faith, we can give these negative thoughts and feelings over to God and know that we have His authority and power to say, like Jesus, "...*not as I will* [not my own natural feelings and desires], *but as Thou wilt.*" (Matthew 26:39) At this point, we can be assured that, since we are a cleansed vessel, God will align our feelings with our faith choice, make us genuine and, then, perform His will through us.

An Example: A Heart Filled with Joy

Here's one last modern day story that exemplifies this principle perfectly. A woman named Sheri wrote me a letter with this incredible story:

> "It was the last day of our trip home to Florida to visit our family and I was at my husband's parents' house where we'd always stayed, packing alone. All the kids were at the beach and Ken, my husband, was out fishing with two brothers-in-law.
>
> "The Lord had me stay home alone and soon I would find out why. As I was packing, the Holy Spirit led me to Ken's suitcase and had me lift up the bottom of the inside of it to find an address book with over two pages of women's names and their descriptions. At

first, I froze, as tears of unbelief welled up deep inside of me. *I wanted to run* (I felt like I had finally found my ticket out of a very unhappy marriage), but the still, small voice of the Spirit of God within constrained me. *'Remember, I'm in control,'* He said. *'How you handle this and the choices you make are critical. Choose to walk by faith, not your feelings, and your life will change.'*

"I called a friend and placed myself under her accountability and received some wise counsel as to how to proceed. My husband arrived home shortly after that and with the book in hand, I asked him if this was happening all over again. He said, 'yes.' He just looked at me and said, 'I am going to hell. You know Jesus, will you please pray for me!'

"Those were perhaps the most honest words I have ever heard him say. So, I did pray and I asked God, 'May *Your* will and not *mine* be done. I give this to You and it is now in Your hands.' (My own feelings inside were screaming, 'run, get out, this is your chance!' But I chose, by faith, to really mean what I had just said in my prayer.)

"Immediately, Ken began to confess everything. He took the book from my hands, ran into the adjoining bathroom and lit it on fire. When he came back he said, 'It is time to expose my sin.'

"A dear pastor that we know came over that night and spent three hours with Ken out in the street. Later, the pastor asked me to come out and told me that 'Ken has just had a Damascus Road experience.' I wouldn't have believed him, except that I had prayed those very same words for my husband many times. And in a prayer meeting just a month earlier, someone gave me a word for my husband, using 'the Damascus Road' analogy. Then the pastor said to me, 'God has heard your prayer. Ken was saved tonight and baptized out in that street.' Well, you can imagine the extreme feelings I was experiencing!

"The next few weeks involved a lot of pain, but an unfolding of the Glory of God like I have never seen before. Ken confessed to all the men he is close to. He confessed to our four teenage children, my mom, sisters and two pastor friends that he was a false convert living a life headed for hell. He even named all his sins, sparing the grossness of the details to protect their imaginations. Telling the children was the hardest of all. They each began to cry. They thought their dad *was* a Christian. But God's glory shone forth, even through this, and He began to heal all of our hearts.

"Eventually, Ken asked me to marry him again and our lives have never been the same. He now calls me from his car and holds the phone up to the marriage tapes he is listening to, so I can hear. For the first time in 19 years, we are experiencing the oneness in the Spirit that God so desires. We are continually in the Word and praying together. We have had more conversation in the past year than we've had in all our 19 years put together. Our children are alive as never before. I didn't realize till now that they, too, were dying.

"There is so much more to share, but God has given me *a heart filled with the joy* that

is born out of pain, a great new love for my
Savior and a hunger to know God's Love in an
even deeper way. Isn't He wonderful!"

Here's a perfect example of how we are not
responsible to change our negative thoughts and
emotions. There's no way we can do that! And,
especially, in a trial like the one above. We're only
responsible to choose to put in charge the Person who
can change our feelings, and that, of course, is God.
And, we do that, by making faith choices to do His
will, regardless of how we feel or what we think. He
then changes our thoughts and emotions to match that
choice.

All of the above stories, Abraham, Joseph, Diana,
the pastor and Sheri are perfect examples of faith
choices. We must not only trust God to perform
through us what He has promised, but we must also
trust Him to make us genuine by aligning our feelings
with what we have chosen.

Identifying With Christ—Obedience and Patient Enduring

How easy it is to simply quote Philippians 3:10 ("That
I may know Him and the power of His resurrection,
and the fellowship of His sufferings, being made
conformable unto His death.") and think we understand
it. However, the more I study this subject, the more I
realize that identifying with Christ in His sufferings
and death is far different than I ever imagined it to
be. It's not only "talking" about Christ's death and
suffering as an objective fact; it's also *personally
experiencing it.* It's picking up our own cross and
choosing His will over our own in every circumstance
we find ourselves. Again, "it's un-learning everything

we have previously learned" in the flesh and learning it, all over again, in the spirit.

As new believers, many of us hastily made claims to identify with Christ's substitutionary death, but most of us were completely unprepared to experience this personally in our own lives. Our identification with Christ needs to include our own personal willingness to fall to the ground and die in every circumstance that God allows, just as John 12:24 says. This is what the fellowship of His suffering is all about.

In a recent newsletter, a pastor comments: "In America today and throughout much of the world, the masses have adopted the Cross, *but have failed to pick it up.* Christ personally promised that true disciples would experience suffering...Suffering is not something inherently bad, but rather a means to achieving the likeness of Christ...it produces perseverance; which leads to, character; which leads to hope... Finally, what's the purpose of suffering? *To bring us to a point where we are not what we were.* Many today aspire to obtain the power of God, the anointing of God and the glory of God, but how many long to partake in the sufferings of God. We must realize that the above can only be obtained through suffering."[54]

That was the way it was with Jesus and that's the way it will be with us.

Only by personally sharing in the likeness of Christ's death can we ever expect to intimately know Him and the power of His resurrection. That's what intimately "knowing God" really means! (Philippians 3:10) But, remember, Scripture promises that, "*after* [we] have suffered awhile, [Christ will] make you *perfect* [complete, whole, mature], strengthened and settled..." (1 Peter 5:10)

Others Can, We May Not

In closing, I'd like to share a wonderful writing with you that has ministered to me over and over again through the hard times. The author is G.D. Watson, who was a Wesleyan Minister back in the 1800s.

"If God has called you to be really like Jesus, He will draw you to a life of crucifixion and humility, and put upon you such demands of obedience that you will not be able to follow other people, or measure yourself by other Christians, and in many ways, He will seem to let other good people do things which He will not let you do.

"Other Christians and ministers who seem very religious and useful may push themselves, pull wires, and work schemes to carry out their plans, but you cannot do it; and if you attempt it, you will meet with such failure and rebuke from the Lord as to make you sorely penitent.

"Others may boast of themselves, of their work, of their success, of their writings, but the Holy Spirit will not allow you to do any such thing, and if you begin it, He will lead you into some deep mortification that will make you despise yourself and all your good works.

"Others may be allowed to succeed in making money, or may have a legacy left to them, but it is likely God will keep you poor, because He wants you to have something far better than gold, namely, a helpless dependence on Him, that He may have the privilege of supplying your needs day by day out of an unseen treasury.

"The Lord may let others be honored and put forward, and keep you hidden in obscurity, because He wants you to produce some choice, fragrant fruit for His coming glory, which can only be produced in the shade. He may let others do a work for Him and get the credit for it, but He will make you work and toil on without knowing how much you are doing, and then to make your work still more precious, He may let others get the credit for the work which you have done, and thus make your reward ten times greater when Jesus comes.

"The Holy Spirit will put a strict watch over you, with a jealous love, and will rebuke you for little words and feelings, or for wasting your time, which other Christians never seem distressed over. So make up your mind that God is an infinite sovereign and has a right to do as He pleases with His own.

"He may not explain to you a thousand things which puzzle your reason in His dealings with you. But if you absolutely sell yourself to be His...slave, He will wrap you up in a jealous love, and bestow upon you many blessings which come only to those who are in the inner circle.

"Settle it forever, then, that you are to deal directly with the Holy Spirit and that He is to have the privilege of tying your tongue, or chaining your hand, or closing your eyes, in ways that He does not seem to use with others. Now when you are so possessed with the living God that you are, in your secret heart, pleased and delighted over this peculiar, personal, private, jealous guardianship and management of the Holy Spirit over your life, you will have found the *vestibule* [entrance] to heaven."

"Finally, be of one mind, having compassion one of another, love as brethren, be pitiful, be courteous: not rendering evil for evil, but on the contrary blessing; knowing that ye are thereunto called, that you should inherit a blessing." (1 Peter 3:9)

Chapter 8
Blessings From *Never Giving Up*

Now that we understand the only way we can endure trials, tribulations and tragedies is by unconditionally trusting God (obeying Him, loving Him, renewing our minds, holding fast to unshakeable faith and "seeing Him" in all things), let's turn our attention to the blessings that result from God's **cycle of trust**:

- Be conformed more into God's image.
- Develop "naked" faith and total dependence upon Him.
- Become "overcomers" in all aspects of the Christian life.
- Experience abundant Life—His Wisdom and Love.
- Experience His presence and intimacy with Him.
- Become true worshippers of God (worshipping Him in the spirit).
- Experience the beauty of His holiness.
- Begin to "see" Him in all things.
- Experience "the peace that passes all understanding."
- Experience the joy of the Lord and <u>all</u> the fruit of the Spirit.
- Experience God's rest.
- Experience His resurrection power.
- Develop Christ-like genuineness and transparency.
- Develop the ability to identify with others.
- Become less judgmental.

Last chapter, we shared some incredible examples of these characteristics. Christians who, rather than succumb to their disappointment, confusion and dismay, allowed those very trials to produce in them patience, experience and hope. (Romans 5:3-4) Most significantly, *they never gave up!* They understood how God wanted them to respond, so their trials could have that "perfect and complete" result that James 1:4 describes. They barred themselves from sin and self and chose, instead, to love and trust God unconditionally. They *lived* Philippians 3:10.

Obedience produces sight, which gives us endurance, which results in blessings.

Let's explore some of these blessings in greater detail:

Overcoming Faith

We have talked much about faith, but we've not really looked at it as a consummate blessing that can result from patiently enduring our trials, tribulation and tragedies. In a trial, our faith can do one of two things: it can (if we allow) grow deeper and deeper or it can "wax cold" and die. The more faith we have, the more it will become apparent to us that God will "never leave us nor forsake us." (Hebrews 13:5) Even though we might not understand what He is doing or why, we'll be able to see His handprint of Love in our lives no matter how black our season of grief is. He will always be there if we are really looking. Remember, my mom's story. Naked faith is *not feeling, not seeing* and *not fully understanding*, but nevertheless, being fully convinced that regardless of what is happening, *God will perform His promises to us in His way and in His timing!*

Read that last statement again. God will be faithful to perform His promises to us *in His way* and *in His timing*. There's the answer. It's His way and His timing, *not our own*!!

Job and Abraham and Moses and Joseph and Paul all had this kind of extreme faith. They always knew it was totally up to God. And they put their total trust in the Lord *despite* their desperate circumstances. They were obedient to love God more than they loved their own lives and as a result, they had the confidence to allow Him to do whatever was necessary to strengthen their faith. The end result in each of their lives magnified God's faithfulness.

The Bible tells us that this kind of trusting faith not only overcomes the world and the flesh, it also overcomes the devil. (1 John 2:13; 5:4) Naked faith repels the enemy. It drives back his hordes and throws off his chains. Consequently, when we lose hope and faith in God, we leave ourselves wide open for Satan's vicious attacks. *The enemy knows that faith and doubt cannot co-exist, therefore he does everything in his power to orchestrate circumstances that make us doubt God's faithfulness.*

This is what's happening in the Christian Body right now. Satan is on an all-out attack, doing all he can in each of our lives to *set us up* for unbelief. If we don't recognize his ploys, if we don't pick up our "Shield of Faith," and if we don't live God's **cycle of trust**, we'll never survive the coming holocaust. Overcoming faith is allowing God to do all that He needs to do in each of our lives, so that we can experience the personal transformation that He is after.

Most Christians today "talk" about *overcoming faith*; we "read" about it and we conduct Bible Studies on it, but if we are really honest with ourselves, very few of us have ever personally experienced it. Most of the time, we walk by the "flesh." And, this is the reason why so many of us don't really know God intimately. Flesh cannot enter God's presence. Pure faith is the only avenue that leads to "seeing Him who is invisible."

2 Corinthians 4:8-9 tells us that even though "we are troubled on every side," we will <u>not</u> be in distress; even though "we are perplexed," we <u>won't</u> be in despair; even though we feel "persecuted" and "cast down," we <u>won't</u> be forsaken or destroyed. And the reason is, *<u>God</u> is holding on to us and <u>we</u> have unconditional faith in Him.*

An Example: Corrie ten Boom's Sister

I love Corrie ten Boom and her stories in *The Hiding Place*. Yet, to me the real heroine of many of her stories, and someone we don't hear too much about, is Corrie's sister, Betsie.

In spite of all the horrific conditions of their imprisonment, Betsie continually chose to *bar herself from following* what she felt, what she wanted and what she needed, and chose instead to do what Christ would have done.

Once, when Betsie was whipped and beaten almost unconscious by a guard and as Corrie was running towards her to help, Betsie screamed out, "Corrie, don't look at my wounds, look only at Jesus!"

Betsie, like so many of us, could have taken that opportunity to "feel sorry for herself" and relish the attention, but instead she denied herself and chose to do what Jesus would do—give her hurts to the Father and look only to Him for His strength.

Another time, towards the end of their imprisonment and after all the hideous things that the German guards had done to them, Corrie turned to Betsie and said, "Don't you hate them for what they have done to us?" Betsie sweetly looked up at her sister and replied, "*Oh, Corrie, what better way to spend our life than to share the gospel with men who need it the most?*"

The lesson we can learn from Betsie is the same one we see in Jesus Himself: "Who, when He was reviled, *reviled not again*; when He suffered, *He threatened not; but committed Himself to Him that judgeth righteously.*" (1 Peter 2:23)

Abundant Life

Another blessing that can result from patiently enduring suffering and trials is the ability to experience abundant life right in the midst of them. Abundant life, again, simply means experiencing God's life—His supernatural Love, wisdom and power—in place of our own (human love, thoughts and desires).

God desires that we all have this kind of abundant, love-filled life right where we are now. John 10:10 declares, "I am come that *they might have life, and that they might have it more abundantly.*" Jesus is not talking about *heavenly* life in this Scripture, but life right here on earth! Abundant life simply means exchanging lives with Christ. We give Him ours; He gives us His. He wants us to have this exchanged life even in the midst of our difficult circumstances. That's the miracle God is after. *Joy, peace, and love come not with the absence of trials, but only with the presence of God.*[55]

Christ not only saves us to show us how much He loves us, He saves us so that we can come to know

Him more and experience His life so as to give it to others. This is what being "conformed into His image" is all about.

Abundant life is experiencing God's Love for someone whom, humanly, we know we can't stand. The imprisoned German pastor is a perfect example of this. In the natural, that pastor hated the sadistic guard, but because he chose to lay down his life and become an open vessel, God gave him His supernatural Love for that guard. In essence, God poured His *Agape* Love through that pastor to the guard.

Not only is *Agape* a part of God's abundant Life, but God's supernatural wisdom is also a part. A perfect example of this is Joseph. Because Joseph chose in his time of need to surrender his natural understanding to the Lord, God gave him His own. Thus, in the situation with his own brothers, with Potiphar's wife and in the situation with the King, Joseph was successful because he relied upon God's wisdom only. He was even able to say to his repentant brothers "you meant it for evil, but God meant it for good." (Genesis 50:20) What human reasoning could ever come up with that?

The third part of God's abundant Life is His supernatural power. What better example of God's miraculous power could we find than Paul? Scripture tells us that he was beaten, put in jail, faced angry mobs, worked to exhaustion, endured sleepless nights and went for days without food. (2 Corinthians 6:4-5; 11:23-27) And yet he lived a powerful life! Why? Because he relied upon God's power within him.

This is what it means to experience abundant life. And, we can have this kind of life even in the midst of our most dismal circumstances. It's always our choice.

"For we who live are always delivered unto death [of self] for Jesus' sake, that the *life also of Jesus* might be made manifest in our mortal flesh." (2 Corinthians 4:11)

An Example: Sarah and Rick

Here's an extreme example of abundant life— God's life through us:

I have a dear, old friend. Yes, we are both old, but my meaning here is that I have known Sarah longer than any of my friends. I think we go back about 40 years!

Sarah is a precious, loyal and wonderful child of God. But about 20 years ago the Lord allowed a heart rending trial into Sarah's life: it was then that she learned that Rick, her husband of 25-30 years, was having an affair with a nurse at his office. (Those of you who have read *The Way of Agape* will remember Sarah's story.) After a year of counseling, a trial separation, yet not much change of heart on Rick's side, they decided to divorce. Sarah, however, because of their children, has all these years remained friendly with Rick.

About five years ago, Rick developed Alzheimer's and quickly deteriorated. At one point, he found himself living alone in a small 20x10 trailer, not able to work, keep a job or shop for himself. My beloved friend, Sarah, prayed intensely about the situation and felt strongly that the Lord wanted her to go over to Rick's every day, fix his meals, clean his trailer and do his shopping for him.

Now, obviously, Sarah was justified by the world's standards to keep her distance and remain unconcerned. After all, <u>he</u> was the one who sinned against her and ruined her life! But, Sarah knew that God wanted her to be an extension of Him and to show Rick unconditional love. So she obediently offered her will and her life to God, saying "God, I can't do this, but You can. I give you me; do what You will."

She began to go over to his trailer daily. At first, she said, it was hard, and she did it purely out of obedience. Yet after a while it became her delight. God went ahead of her, prepared her heart and filled her with His Love for Rick.

It's been five years now, and my precious Sarah is still taking care of Rick. She has moved him into her home to make it easier for her to care for him. She must do almost everything for him now, but because of her sacrifice, they have, once again, become friends. Their two grown children are amazed at what has happened, but are delighted to see their two parents finally getting together again. It's a miraculous story and one that's absolutely true. But it's only because beautiful Sarah said to the Lord, "*My Jesus, I offer all that I am to You. I surrender my will and my life. May all that pleases You and all that You wish, happen...*"

Scripture calls these kinds of sacrifices, the "sacrifice of praise" (Hebrews 13:15), the "sacrifice of righteousness" (Psalm 4:5) and the "sacrifice of thanksgiving" (Psalm 116:17; 107:22). These are called 'sacrifices' because, much of the time, we really don't "feel" like praising Him, being thankful or joyful, but, by faith, we do it anyway because He has told us to. Sarah is a beautiful example of this "living sacrifice."

Intimacy

One of the most precious blessings that can come from patiently enduring trials and difficulties is the intimacy we develop with the Lord. When all other crutches have been taken away and, yet we still choose to lay ourselves down before the Lord, the intimacy that results is like nothing we have ever experienced. Intimacy simply means an all pervasive awareness of His presence, no matter what our circumstances are. Everywhere we go, no matter how far, we know He is with us. Nothing in the world compares with this knowledge. Intimacy is where God *teaches, guides and communes with us* and we, in turn, *worship, praise and love Him.* We learn this kind of intimacy only through complete trust in the Lord.

Many Christians, unfortunately, have settled for a pale imitation of Christianity. They declare they are willing to pay the price for deeper intimacy with God, but when God begins to rearrange their lives through trials, tribulations and tragedies, they writhe in agony. Until we are willing to let our precious alabaster boxes be completely broken and Jesus' life formed in us, we will never fully experience the fulness and the oneness with God that the Bible indicates. Trials are simply Father-filtered periods of time where He purposely puts us into a corner, so that we'll have no other choice but to depend totally upon Him.

An Example: Diana

A perfect example of one who not only experienced abundant life but who also enjoyed the most profound intimacy with the Lord, was, again, my dear friend Diana Bandtlow, whom we spoke about last chapter.

As you recall, Diana was only two years old in the Lord when she was diagnosed with leukemia and given only six months to live. But no matter what the circumstances were, no matter how much pain she was in, she continually chose to lay her life down to the Lord because *she knew that He loved her* and that He wouldn't allow anything into her life that wasn't "Father-filtered."

She was invited to teach a Bible study those last six months of her life. Now, if it had been you or I, we probably would have spent those precious months at home with our families. Remember, Diana had a husband who adored her and two beautiful little children, Hillary, 3, and Stephanie, 1. But not Diana. She prayed about it and felt strongly that God wanted her out there sharing with her friends exactly what He was doing in her life. That little Bible study grew to about 50 people, because everyone around her saw an intimacy with God that none of us had. At that time, I had been a Christian for about 15 years, and yet I had never met anyone like Diana. It was apparent to all of us that she knew God on a level that none of us had ever experienced.

Diana's leukemia was diagnosed in June, and by November she was permanently confined to the hospital. At Thanksgiving, I wanted desperately to give her something to show her how much I loved her and how much she had ministered to my life.

In a gift store, I found a cute bird's nest, all done in fall colors with two little sparrows in it. I just knew it was for Diana. I quickly bought it and raced home. In the car on the way home, the Scripture that came to me was Matthew 10:29-31, "Are not two sparrows sold for a farthing? And one of them shall not fall on the ground without your Father. But the very hairs of your head are all numbered. Fear not, therefore, ye are of more value than many sparrows."

Well, I was excited because the Scripture fit so perfectly. I wrote it on a card, put it with the nest, and asked Chuck when he got home to deliver it to the hospital for me.

About a half an hour later, Diana called and said, "Oh Nancy, I love the bird's nest! I know it's from God because He always tells me not to fear! But," she said, "what you don't know, and what no one else knows—except for God—is that I am losing all my hair. And God tells me right here that *He loves me so much that 'all the hairs on my head are numbered' to Him.*"

Now, I had no way of knowing that was happening. I had not seen Diana in three months. Yet, God knew and had communicated His Love to her through that Scripture. That's our faithful and loving Father who is interested and concerned about every detail of our lives and who yearns to have an intimate relationship with every one of us.

Trials have a way of jump-starting this intimacy— if we allow them to! Obedience produces sight, which results in endurance and the blessing of His presence.

Another Example: "A Million Prayers"

I introduced you to my dear friend, Liz, in Chapter Four. She's the one who had "stage four" cancer and coerced her doctors into letting her leave the hospital for a few hours every Saturday in order to attend a faith seminar in a neighboring city.

Jim, Liz's husband, went shopping with her for four wigs, five hats and several scarves to cover her head since her doctor had "guaranteed" the chemo would result in the eventual loss of her hair. Three of the wigs were for everyday, but the fourth was a special order through her hairdresser who had considerable experience helping other cancer patients. She suggested that Liz have the new wig shipped by the quickest method, as it appeared she would lose all her hair before it would arrive by regular mail. When her hair began to fall out, as was expected, Liz found the Scripture we mentioned in the above example with Diana, "Are not two sparrows sold for a farthing? And one of them shall not fall on the ground without your Father. *But the very hairs of your head are all numbered.* Fear not, therefore, ye are of more value than many sparrows." (Matthew 10:29-31)

Liz took that Scripture literally. Since we "are of more value than many sparrows," she decided to ask God for "a million prayers to be granted" for each hair that she lost. She believes that she shocked Satan out of his boots, because immediately her hair stopped falling out and she never had to wear those four wigs, five hats or several scarves. My precious Liz now says, she feels that she "limited God" by asking for *only* a million prayers. She feels that rather than stipulating the conditions, she should have given it unconditionally to God to do according to His will, trusting in Him who knows our hearts, and not limiting His limitless powers.

The Scripture from Job 13:15, "Though You slay me, yet will I trust You," describes my dear Liz perfectly.

Loving Others

Besides naked faith, abundant life and intimacy with the Father, another wonderful result of longsuffering in trials is the ability to experience God's unconditional Love for others. Because we have personally experienced God's Love during our trial, we can now turn around and share that Love with someone else.

God desires that our trials produce in us a broken, humble and willing heart where His Love can freely flow. It did through Diana. It did through the German Pastor. And, it can through us also. We know it's His Love, and because we are now cleansed vessels it can flow freely through us.

1 Peter 1:22 sums up what loving others really means: "Seeing that ye have purified your souls in obeying the truth through the Spirit unto unfeigned Love [*Agape*] of the brethren, *see that ye love* [*agapao*] one another with a pure heart fervently."

Until we are willing to have our souls searched and cleansed, however, we won't be able to genuinely love others. In reality, there is no way we can "totally give ourselves over to" another person, until we have *first* learned to "totally give ourselves over to" God. Remember, the First and Second Commandments must go in the order they were given. We cannot love others as ourselves until we have *first* learned to love God. (Matthew 22:37-39) As we said in Chapter Two, only God can make loving others genuinely possible. Again, it's His Love. He just needs an empty vessel to pour it through. Trials have a way of teaching us how to do become such a vessel.

Christians who are unwilling to love God first, will not be able to experience His Love for others. They will be "closed off" vessels—filled with self, not God. And, we've seen this result from trials and tragedies. Rather than become more loving towards others, many Christians become angry, bitter and desirous that others pay for what they have experienced.

When we begin to love God's way, however—loving others as or instead of ourselves—all men are going to know, <u>not</u> by what we "say" but by how we "live," that we truly are Christians. John 13:35 confirms this, *"By this shall all men know that ye are My disciples, if ye have love one to another."*

"Herein is our Love made perfect, that we may have boldness in the day of judgment, *because as He is, so are we in this world."* (1 John 4:17) In this same chapter, John tells us that Love is the very nature of God!

Again, if we have been obedient and yielding, trials can produce these glorious results in us.

Being Extensions of His Love

God's Love doesn't just fall down from heaven, it must be passed on through us. We are His "arms and legs" of Love in this world. *We are extensions of His Love,* <u>if</u> we so choose to be. All that is required of us is a cleansed life.

Now, being extensions of God's Love doesn't really sound too complicated or too difficult. Why, then, is there not more of His Love being passed on in the Christian body today? If Jesus is in us and we have His Love in our hearts, then why are we having such a hard time loving others as God would have us to do? Matthew 24:12 gives us the answer. It says that in the end times, "because iniquity shall abound, *the Love [Agape] of many shall wax cold."*

Well, trials have a way of reversing this, if we allow them to!

Moses is a perfect example. As a child, he was pampered, smothered and constantly cared for by others. As a young man, he was absorbed in his own needs. And as a prince, he didn't have to think about anyone else but himself. However, after he suffered separation from his family and flight as a fugitive and a murderer, his focus radically changed! He became totally broken and very much concerned about others. Now, God could really begin to use him.

Before, Moses was very powerful, very rich and very visible. He was also unapproachable, distant and aloof. But, after enduring his trials, he became humble, accessible, and able to identify with others' needs.

The personal experience of suffering and patient endurance has a way of bringing our real priorities back into focus.

Identifying with Others

Following along with this same principle of being extensions of God's Love, enduring our own trials enables us to identify with others who are also experiencing the same kind of difficulties. This was true in Moses' life; it's also true in our own. Trials have a way of making us more transparent and open with our *own* problems. I remember one gentleman, years ago, who refused to read any of my books because, he said, I was a "millionaire," and he was sure I could never understand what he was experiencing. It wasn't until we, ourselves, went through total and complete bankruptcy and the loss of everything, that he finally wrote back and said, "Okay, *now* let's hear what you have to say."

I fully understood what he meant. We cannot completely identify with another's problems unless we ourselves have experienced something similar. We must have "been there" in order to really be able to relate to what they are going through. This is one of the things I've noticed that non-believers pick up about Christians. We have a habit of "preaching" when we come across someone in trouble, rather than simply listening to learn where they are coming from. Often we don't have the faintest idea what those people are experiencing, yet we feel we must give them the Gospel. What they really need is for someone to hold them, love them and encourage them. Action and time are what count, not just words; words are so easy. What they want to know and see is: will you put your feet where your mouth is? Will you become an extension of God's Love? They need to "see" and "feel" the Love of God through us. Once we establish a relationship, there will be an appropriate time to share the Gospel. But it's our actions that first open a person's heart.

Therefore, unless we ourselves have gone through something similar, we truly don't understand what they are experiencing. As Scripture says, we can only encourage the fainthearted *with the "comfort that* <u>*we*</u> *have received" in going through the same thing ourselves*.

2 Corinthians 1:3 reminds us: "Blessed be God, even the Father of our Lord Jesus Christ, the Father of mercies, and the God of all comfort, who comforteth us in all our tribulation, that we may be able to comfort them who are in any trouble, *by the comfort with which we ourselves are comforted of God.*"

I am really passionate about this point! Perhaps it's because I have experienced both sides of the issue. All of my books over the past 25 years have simply been a chronology of my own walk with the Lord and what He has done in my life. But I am only able to share and minister what I, myself, have experienced.

There are still many areas where I have not been: I don't know what it's like to be chronically ill, or to lose a husband or have a crippled child. These are areas I would never presume to minister in, but simply to hold and love and encourage.

Enduring similar trials has a way of producing empathy within us, helping us identify with others.

Becoming Good Listeners

Again, following the same thought of being able to identify with others, patiently enduring trials has a way of making us "good listeners," not just good talkers. Because we have been there ourselves, we know that those in trouble don't need preaching, but simply a sympathetic ear and someone willing to pray.

Furthermore, we'll know from experience that we, as comforters, don't need to have all the "answers." Often, there simply are no answers! Horrific trials, tribulation and tragedies often scare Christians. Not only are they scared to go through them personally, they are also scared to minister to those experiencing them. Some of the reactions I hear are: "I just don't know what to say to her," or "I don't know the Bible well enough to minister to him," etc. Thus, these Christians back off, become silent and then, avoid those in need. Most do not realize that what those in trouble really need is just someone to say, "I care. What can I do for you?" Hurting Christians certainly don't need clichés or frail answers, but simply someone to hold them and tell them they are loved. Or to clean their house for them. Or take their kids to school. Be creative. Do something *for* them.

Having endured trials ourselves has a way of making us *more supersensitive to others' needs*. It also gives us the impetus to reach out first. God's Love is initiating Love, which means it's the first to reach out. It takes the first step and when we choose to love with God's Love, He not only gives us the Love we need but also the ability to initiate that Love to others.

God wants each of us humble enough, sensitive enough and attentive enough, so that when He prompts us, we can initiate His Love to someone He knows desperately needs it. Since we have been in the same predicament, we know how vital it is to have someone simply say, "I care."

An Example:

Years ago in one of my seminars, there was a severely overweight 21-year old, who always sat in the back row, almost out of sight. She never spoke to anyone and no one ever spoke to her. She never smiled. Her pretty face was always sullen and withdrawn.

God laid this girl so heavily on my heart that after one of the sessions, I went up to her and said, "Hey, let's go and have lunch together." Surprised that I was talking to her, she turned around as if I meant someone else behind her. You could see on her face that she was convinced I certainly didn't mean her. "*You* and I!" I said. I took her by the hand and led her to the coffee shop.

At first it was very difficult to get her to talk, but once started, I couldn't stop her. I could tell that it had been a long, long time since she had felt God's Love through anyone. What do you think this young girl's self-image was built upon? Do you think it was built upon God's Love and what He thought of her? No way! Her self-image was totally built upon what she thought of herself and upon what *she thought* others thought of her.

I know this young woman experienced God's Love that day, because at the very next session there she was, sitting in the front row, wearing a great big smile. That night we had an "afterglow" meeting, and this precious girl recommitted her life to Christ. She told us later that she had been backslidden for three years, because she had not experienced Love from anyone. God, however, opened her up that day and loved this precious child right back to Himself.

I am convinced that *God's Love comes through us*, His body. *Each of us is God's arms and legs in this world.* We are *extensions of His Love*!

God wants us to be doers of His Word, not hearers only.

Being Genuine and Real

Another wonderful result of longsuffering, is the ability to be real and genuine with each other. Patient endurance has a way of removing our phoniness and our hypocrisy. It strips away our facades and everything becomes exposed. Trials, in themselves, help us to become vulnerable. Now, I know being vulnerable can be scary; but the reality of it is, any time we "love" we're vulnerable. And God commands us to love, thus to be vulnerable.

Sharing our own experiences of being downcast and hurt by others, also allows us to tell how God touched us and stood us back up on our feet. Now, we don't need to dwell on the negative details of the past, but share just enough so others can identify with us. Concentrate on what the Lord has done, is doing and will be doing in the future. This is what they need to hear!

Being genuine and real with others does *not* mean being *perfect*. Far from it! "Perfect people" are not touchable people, because no one can really identify with them. We are all sinners and, as Scripture says, "There is none righteous, no, not one." (Romans 3:10) Therefore, as Christians, *we are not to strive to be self-righteously "perfect," but only real and genuine, pointing others to the only One who is perfect—and that One, of course, is Jesus.*

Again, Dietrich Bonhoeffer had this to say: "To be conformed with the Incarnate—that is to be a real man. It is man's right and duty that he should be a man...The real man is not an object either for contempt or for deification, but an object of the love of God...The real man is at liberty to be his creator's creature. To be conformed with the incarnate is to have the right to be the man one really is. Then *there is no more pretense, no more hypocrisy or self-violence, no more compulsion to be something other, better, and more ideal than what one really is. God loves the real man. God became a real man.*"

This point was brought home to me recently when someone shared with me, "One of the things I can't stand about 'Christians' is that they put on such an air of being perfect." He then went on to declare, "I just can't relate to them." I understood exactly what he was saying because I, too, remember as a young Christian seeing some of the speakers at our church "float in" in their long white robes and feeling that I never could identify with them. They appeared to have it "all together." Even back then, they seemed so unreal to me.

This is one of the reasons why I love David in the Old Testament so much. I can identify with him. He blew it, just as I do. He failed. And, he missed the mark. Yet God called him "a man after His own heart."[56] David experienced things I experience. He went through all the temptations I go through. And if God called him "a man after His own heart," then there's hope for me. David comforts me in his psalms "by the comfort he received from God" when he was going through his hard times.

Genuineness and realness are another result of longsuffering. I've found that the more intimate and transparent I can be with the Father in the prayer closet, the more open and honest I can be with others.

Admitting the Truth

Only a humble and broken person can admit his own need, and admit that he can't live the Christian life on his own. That's all humility is—simply admitting the truth about oneself. If our *security* is in Jesus and in His Love for us, then we'll be able to be honest and transparent. Because we have personally experienced difficulties in our own life, the truth has probably come out, anyway, and thus we've had to embrace it. There's no more covering it up; it's out there in living color.

I really believe if more Christians could learn the principles of humility, transparency and truthfulness, we would see the non-believing world rushing to know Christ. Our realness would bring them in. They would be able to see *Christ in us*. It's our Christian pride, hypocrisy and phoniness that repels them.

The Apostle Paul was obviously one of the most mature and Spirit-filled Christians in the entire Bible. Yet, he admitted, in 2 Corinthians 1:8, that he had such huge problems that he despaired even of life itself. The way Paul handled these problems, however, was not to cover them up or pretend they didn't exist, but "*to boast in his infirmities*" and in his human frailties. He knew that God loved him no matter what happened, and that allowed him to be open and honest with others. He also knew that God would, somehow, work all things together for good in his life.[57] (2 Corinthians 12:9-10)

Paul's identity and security were so completely wrapped up in Jesus Christ that he was able to continually say, "For to me to live is Christ." (Philippians 1:21) This is what we must continually remind ourselves of. *It's not I, but Christ in us.*

Longsuffering has a way of highlighting these things, and when we learn them, they can become blessings.

An Example: Transparency is Contagious

Nothing will cause the masks of others to come down faster than being real, honest, and touchable, pointing others to Christ. As one young woman said to me recently, "Nancy, *being transparent is contagious!*"

In one *Way of Agape* seminar many years ago, some of the women came up to me privately and shared how they had tremendous anger and resentment towards others in their church body. It was a little frightening, because there seemed to be so many hurts and divisions in this particular church.

At the end of the three-day seminar, we all gathered together to share what we had learned personally. God prompted one sister in the front row to stand up and publicly ask forgiveness from a woman in the back row of the auditorium. The first lady said she had been holding resentment and bitterness towards the other woman for years. The woman in the back row was so overcome by God's Love that she, too, stood and asked forgiveness. She was crying, as she, too, admitted to being consumed in bitterness.

Then all over the audience, women began to stand and share their hurts and ask for Love. One woman in leadership, who looked like the most "put together" person there, shared how it was all an act and how really scared and lonely she was. She humbled herself and asked for love from all of us.

After the class was over, we stayed for three hours sharing and praying and hugging and loving. It was one of the most rewarding of all the seminars I've ever given, because God broke down those prideful and arrogant and self-centered walls and masks, and the truth was able to come forth. Self was exposed; women were broken and set free.

How appropriate it is that one of the definitions of longsuffering is that it is a means of *un-selfing* us. God wants us united in Him. It's our self-life that separates us. If we can learn to *get rid of our self-life, then, just watch our churches become united in God's Love*!

Again, longsuffering has a way of exposing our self-life in living color. (A blessing we need to embrace... and what a blessing it can be!)

Love, Don't Judge One Another

Another blessing we can learn from patiently enduring our trials and not falling back, is to love one another and not judge one another. What's amazing to me is how tolerant we become of others, after we ourselves have experienced a similar situation. It seems *we learn not to judge one another by experiencing others judging us!*

Now, of course, this can also back fire! We can become judgmental and more hardened and more unloving because of our trials. We've all seen this result. But the consequences of this way of thinking are tragic. We end up cutting off all communication with the Lord and quenching His Spirit at a time we need to hear from Him the most. Stifling our communication at this point can be disastrous.

Going through our own times of trial and suffering, we learn that God is the only One who can rightfully judge. He is the only One who can see our hearts and knows the truth. Therefore, when we look at people who "appear" to be spiritual or appear <u>not</u> to be spiritual, we must learn not to judge them. *We* don't really know. Only He does!

Here's a classic example:

A woman came to one of my early seminars (I had only been teaching for a few months), sat right in the middle of the front row, and after five minutes of the study promptly fell asleep. After several weeks of this behavior, I found myself becoming quite angry at her. "Why does she even come if she is going to fall asleep? And if she wants to sleep, why does she have to sit right in the middle of the front row?"

Since I was still quite new at teaching and therefore, very insecure, I found her to be a real distraction. When I would look out into the audience, trying to make a particular point, there she was sound asleep in the front row. This made me totally lose my train of thought and think to myself, "Is what I am saying so boring?"

Finally, after about the fourth time this happened, I went to the women in charge and 'subtly' asked them about her. "Oh," they said, "Nan, don't worry about her. She needs this study more than anyone else, and she is loving it! *She has a physical impairment of the eyes which prevents her from looking into bright lights, but she hasn't missed a thing that you have said!"*

God said to me that day, "Nancy Missler, you are **not** to judge what I am doing in someone else's heart by what you see or by what you think." He showed me that had I prayed about her and not complained about her, He would have assured me of His purpose for her.

Now, when I go to churches to speak, and perhaps, at first glance, the body *appears* cold or unfriendly or unloving, I don't question God anymore as to *why* He sent me. I can almost hear His answer, "It's none of your business *why* I sent you here; just do what I have called you to do and I will handle the rest!" If we do our part, He will assuredly do His.

Again, *obedience produces sight, which enables us to endure and results in blessing.*

In Conclusion

We spoke in Chapter Six about the eagle and how he "weathers the storms" by keeping his eyes upon the sun. Instead of succumbing to the storm, he actually allows it to push him to safety and freedom and peace. Well, it's the same with us. We can experience "a peace that passes all understanding" in the midst of our storm if we understand how to patiently endure, if we understand how to unconditionally trust the Lord, and if we are living His **cycle of trust**. Personally knowing His will and His Love produces a willingness in us to obey Him in all things, which will result in our being able to see Him and endure all that He allows.

Now, again, it's <u>not</u> that all our trials, tribulations and tragedies will go away when we understand these things; but, by doing them, we <u>will</u> be able to have **victory in the eye of the storm** just like that eagle. The storms and trials in our lives will <u>not</u> have overcome us but actually empowered us into the presence of Jesus!

Thus, rather than being "lost" in our times of testing as we might feel, we actually are found. *God has been working to clear away the debris in our lives, so that He can bring about a relationship with Him that we have never before known.* A relationship where we patiently endure all the circumstances that He sends and *never give up*. And, because of that, we will develop a stronger faith; enjoy abundant life and intimacy with Him; learn genuine love and identity with others, not judging them; become real and transparent and experience a peace that passes all understanding.

It's called longsuffering, fruit of the end times.

Longsuffering is the pinnacle of living God's **cycle of trust**. Because we know His will and His Love, and we have unconditionally obeyed and trusted Him, He has manifested Himself to us and given us the fortitude to endure all things. We have come to know that no matter what happens, *He will never leave us nor forsake us*. And, like Job, we can say and mean, "I had heard of Thee by the hearing of the ear, but <u>now</u> *mine eye seeth Thee*." (Job 42:5)

Love never gives up!

End Notes

1. *Dietrich Bonhoeffer*, Michael Van Dyke, Barbour Books, 2001.
2. 1 Corinthians 1:23
3. Matthew 16:24
4. *Dietrich Bonhoeffer*, Michael Van Dyke, Barbour Books, 2001, page 113-116.
5. *Dietrich Bonhoeffer*, Michael Van Dyke, pages 68-69.
6. *Times Square Pulpit Series*, David Wilkerson, "Are You Mad at God?" 2/16/98.
7. Exodus 2:23; Isaiah 63:9; Judges 10:16; Exodus 2:24-25
8. Exodus 6:6-8
9. Psalm 77:2; 119:67
10. 2 Chronicles 33:12
11. Ephesians 1:17-20; 1 Corinthians 2:9
12. Psalm 119:71
13. 1 Peter 5:10
14. She "sang in the spirit" just as 1 Corinthians 14:15 says we can.
15. Jeremiah 10:23; Isaiah 40:28
16. For clarification: If we are Christians, then the Holy Spirit is the source, the origin and the beginning of our minds. However, if Satan can sever, quench or thwart God's control, by simply causing us to choose to follow our own emotional way of thinking, then Satan will end up directing our lives through the "flesh."
17. Romans 7:15,19
18. Romans 7:25
19. Matthew 18:32-33; Colossians 3:13
20. Dietrich Bonhoeffer, page 205.
21. Romans 8:28
22. *One Who Believed*, Dr. Robert B. Pamplin, pages 5-6.
23. Psalm 88, Job 16:12-16; Job 7:20; Psalm 18:5-6
24. Psalms 139:7-8, 12
25. Judges 6:13

26. Victorious Christian Faith, Alan Redpath, page 14.

27. Hebrews 10:38
28. Hebrews 11:11
29. Spirit of Heaviness—depression (Isaiah 61:3): Sorrow-grief (Nehemiah 2:2; Proverbs 15:13); Broken Heart (Psalm 69:20; Proverbs 18:14; Despair-hopelessness (2 Corinthians 1:8-9); Inner Hurts (Luke 4:18; Proverbs 26:22).
30. Colossians 3:5; Galatians 5:24; Ephesians 4:22
31. Taken, in part, from *Parables*, "Bulletin and Newsletter Series," Winter 98.
32. Genesis 32:30
33. Exodus 14:13-14; Deuteronomy.8:2; Psalm 46:10
34. Romans 6:13
35. Ephesians 3:20; Matthew 7:9-11
36. Psalms 18:1-6; 30:2-3; 55:16-18; 81:7
37. Isaiah 50:10
38. Psalm 66:9
39. Hebrews 13:8
40. Romans 12:19
41. Psalms 5:11; 18:47; 89:18; Isaiah 35:4
42. Deuteronomy 20:4
43. 1 Samuel 24:17
44. Ephesians 6:11, 13
45. Hebrews 13:15; Psalm 100
46. Psalms 107:22; 116:17; 95:2; 69:30
47. Romans 8:28
48. Colossians 1:17
49. Isaiah 45:7
50. Romans 12:19
51. Victorious Christian Living, Alan Redpath, page 15.
52. This was sent to me by E-mail from someone who thought it was by George MacDonald.
53. John 8:36
54. World Ministries International, Rev. Jonathan Hansen 5/03
55. Psalm 16:11
56. Acts 13:22
57. Romans 8:28

Pathway to the Garden Tomb

Garden at the Tomb

Garden at the Tomb

Plain & Simple Series

The Key
HOW TO LET GO AND LET GOD

This book teaches us the moment-by-moment steps to letting go of ourselves, our circumstances and others and *putting on Christ*. It gives us a practical guide to giving our problems to God and leaving them there. One of our most popular books.

Why Should I be the First to Change?
THE KEY TO A LOVING MARRIAGE

This is the story of the amazing "turnaround" of Chuck and Nancy's 20-year Christian marriage which reveals the dynamic secret that releases the power of God's Love already resident in every believer. Riveting, yet easy reading.

Tomorrow May Be Too Late
DISCOVERING OUR DESTINY

A simple, non-threatening and easy to read book that chronicles God's whole plan for mankind. In just a little over a hundred pages, it relates man's spiritual journey from the beginning of time to the very end, showing how God has been personally and intimately involved all along. Perfect for non-believers.

The Choice
HYPOCRISY OR REAL CHRISTIANITY

As Christians, we are faced with a constant choice: either to live our Christian life in our own power and ability, or to set ourselves aside and let Christ live His Life out through us. Written especially for youth.

Against the Tide
GETTING BEYOND OURSELVES

This little book gives the practical tools we need to implement "faith choices" in our lives. These are choices that set aside our natural thoughts and emotions, and allow us to love and be loved as God desires. Great for understanding emotions.

KHW

What is
The King's High Way?

The King's *High* Way is a ministry dedicated to encouraging and teaching Christians how to walk out their faith, i.e., focusing on the practical application of Biblical principles. Our passion is to help believers learn how to love as Jesus loved; how to renew their minds so their lives can be transformed; and, how to have unshakeable faith in their night seasons. Isaiah 62:10 is our commission: helping believers walk on the King's *High* Way by gathering out the stumbling blocks and lifting up the banner of Jesus.

For more information, please write to:

The King's *High* Way
P.O. Box 3111
Coeur d' Alene, Idaho 83816

or call:
1-866-775-KING

On the Internet:
http://www.kingshighway.org